NATIONAL DEFENSE RESEARCH INSTITUTE

T0308518

Improving the Timeliness of Equal Employment Opportunity Complaint Processing in Department of Defense

Miriam Matthews, Nelson Lim

Prepared for the Office of Diversity Management and Equal Opportunity

For more information on this publication, visit www.rand.org/t/rr680

Library of Congress Cataloging-in-Publication Data
ISBN: 978-0-8330-8803-1

Published by the RAND Corporation, Santa Monica, Calif.
© Copyright 2015 RAND Corporation
RAND® is a registered trademark.

Cover image: Stopwatch closeup, Fotolia@Aaron Amat; Seal, courtesy of DoD

Support RAND
Make a tax-deductible charitable contribution at
www.rand.org/giving/contribute

www.rand.org

Preface

The Offices of Diversity Management and Equal Opportunity and Civilian Personnel Policy aim to provide a work environment in which all Department of Defense (DoD) employees are provided equal employment opportunities regardless of their diverse backgrounds. When an individual believes that he or she has been discriminated against, the aggrieved person can contact an Equal Employment Opportunity (EEO) office and may elect to formally file a complaint in DoD regarding the discrimination. Once a person files a formal EEO complaint, federal regulations stipulate that, barring specific circumstances, the complaint should be processed within 180 days. For years, the majority of EEO complaints filed in DoD have not been processed within this regulated time frame.

This report aims to provide information that will assist DoD in addressing this delay of formal EEO complaints. It describes assessments of the trends and root causes associated with the lack of EEO complaint processing timeliness, and it identifies several potential avenues for improving processing timeliness. It also outlines a method for systematically evaluating the effects of changes that DoD may make to its complaint processing procedures.

The research was sponsored by the Office of Diversity Management and Equal Opportunity in the Office of the Secretary of Defense and conducted within the Forces and Resources Policy Center of the RAND National Defense Research Institute, a federally funded research and development center sponsored by the Office of the Secretary of Defense, the Joint Staff, the Unified Combatant Commands, the Navy, the Marine Corps, the defense agencies, and the defense Intelligence Community. For more information on the RAND Forces and Resources Policy Center, see http://www.rand.org/nsrd/ndri/centers/frp.html or contact the director (contact information is provided on the web page).

Contents

Figures and Tables

Figures

Tables

Summary

The Department of Defense (DoD) employs hundreds of thousands of full-time civilian employees, and federal laws and executive orders stipulate that it is illegal to discriminate against these persons on the basis of several protected categories, including race, color, religion, sex, age, national origin, and disability. The Offices of Diversity Management and Equal Opportunity (ODMEO) and Civilian Personnel Policy aim to ensure that DoD abides by these laws and orders, thereby allowing DoD civilian employees to work in an environment that is free from discrimination.

If a DoD civilian employee perceives that he or she has been discriminated against, the employee can contact the local Equal Employment Opportunity (EEO) office to discuss the discrimination experience(s). The office will explore potential avenues that may help to resolve the issues that are raised. If the complaint cannot be immediately resolved, the individual may subsequently file a formal EEO complaint with the local EEO office. Between 2,500 and 3,000 EEO complaints are formally filed in DoD on an annual basis. Once a person files a formal EEO complaint, federal regulations stipulate that, barring specific circumstances, the complaint should be processed within 180 days. This 180-day time period encompasses the time of formal filing to the time an EEO office mails the report of investigation (ROI) for the complaint to the complainant.

Since at least 2005, 38 percent to 53 percent of EEO complaints filed each year in DoD have not been processed within this regulated 180-day time frame. When complaint processing exceeds 180 days,

DoD is in violation of federal regulations and at risk of sanctions from the EEOC for discrimination based on procedural issues, and the employee who filed the complaint may continue to work in a discriminatory environment. This report aims to provide information that will assist DoD in addressing this lag of formal EEO complaints.

Research Approach

To better understand current formal EEO complaint processing in DoD, we pursued several lines of research:

1. We reviewed a previous evaluation of EEO complaint processing within DoD.
2. We obtained and analyzed information from administrative databases in order to examine the trends in formal EEO complaints across DoD and other federal agencies. To identify the case characteristics associated with untimeliness, we analyzed case history data maintained by the Investigations and Resolutions Division (IRD) of the Civilian Personnel Policy/Defense Civilian Personnel Advisory Service. IRD is an agency within DoD that investigates and mediates complaints for DoD components, including the Army, Air Force, and Navy.
3. We conducted interviews with directors and key personnel, including investigators, intake personnel, and quality assurance personnel, in IRD. We also conducted interviews with EEO directors and key personnel in the Army, Navy, and Air Force.

Findings and Recommendations

Building from these analyses and discussions, we identified certain avenues that DoD should pursue to improve the timeliness of the EEO complaint process.

Continue to Address Case Backlog Through "Blitzing"

Interviews and discussions with IRD personnel and military service personnel involved with the EEO process revealed concerns that a sharp increase in the number of cases received by IRD was contributing to difficulties in processing EEO complaint cases in a timely manner. Interviewees described a process known as "blitzing" that is sometimes used to quickly work through several cases at a specific installation. Specifically, installations that have seven or more cases have been considered as candidates for this blitz process. When an installation participates in a blitz, it collects all necessary documentation and schedules interviews with all relevant individuals during a limited time frame. Then one or more IRD investigators visit the installation in person and rapidly process the cases.

Those involved with the blitzes spoke positively about the ability of this process to increase the rapidity of investigations. Indeed, blitzing the cases may help with quickly reducing backlog and preventing continued backlog. To permit locations with a smaller number of submitted complaints to participate in the blitz process, increased utilization of a centralized blitzing process should be pursued. Under a centralized blitzing process, different installations or activities that are in geographic proximity with one another may all collect relevant documentation and schedule relevant interviews close together. This may allow one or more investigators to rapidly process cases that, although not at the same location, are near to one another.

Require Management Participation in Alternative Dispute Resolution

Another way to reduce backlog is to reduce the number of cases that go to or continue through the formal investigation process. One way to do this is through the use of alternative dispute resolution (ADR). When individuals contact their EEO office to make a discrimination complaint, an EEO counselor may offer the option of ADR. ADR can involve a number of different techniques, including mediation, use of an ombudsman, peer review, fact finding, early neutral evaluation, a settlement conference, facilitation, or a mini-trial. The specific resolutions offered vary on a case-by-case basis.

Several of our interviewees spoke highly of ADR as a way to resolve complaints in a timely manner. However, they also told us that one obstacle to its increased use is that some complainants and managers within DoD components resist its use. We recommend that all DoD agencies require management to participate in ADR when it has been offered to the complainant and the complainant has agreed to participate.[1] If lower-level management refuses to do so, they must provide an explanation for refusal to participate in ADR to higher-level management. Higher-level management should then participate instead. Thus, required management participation would involve participating in the ADR process or provision of explanation to higher-level management for refusal to participate.

Increase Accountability and Standardization of Data and Document Submission Through Use of Checklists

A major theme that emerged in our interviews was that time is required to obtain the needed data and documentation for incomplete EEO complaint cases that are submitted to IRD with requests for investigation. Interviewees also noted confusion regarding what to submit with a particular case, and our analysis of administrative databases showed that cases spent a lengthy period of time with IRD intake.

The IRD provides a list of required and recommended materials on its website, but EEO personnel within the military services access the IRD site and use these document lists with variability. Further, even when complete cases are submitted to IRD for investigation, documentation already included with the case files is frequently requested by IRD intake staff.

To reduce incomplete case submission and document requests for cases that have been submitted complete, increased accountability and standardization of data and document submission is needed. To accomplish this, IRD should require submission of checklists with requests for investigation. The RAND team, working with IRD, has already developed these checklists (which vary based on the type of complaint being submitted), and they are provided in the appendix, available separately online at http://www.rand.org/pubs/research_reports/RR680.

---

[1]   The agency and the complainant must knowingly and willingly enter into ADR. If ADR is offered by the agency, this represents the agency's willingness to participate, and thus, management should acknowledge this.

These checklists require EEO personnel to indicate which documents have and have not been submitted, and they also require personnel to attach their names to the document submission.

However, systematic implementation and evaluation of EEO complaint processing changes should be practiced. Therefore, before requiring the use of checklists, DoD should conduct a randomized control trial (RCT) to assess the effectiveness of checklist use in reducing complaint processing times. This is discussed in more detail below.

Employ Experienced or Well-Trained Personnel for IRD Intake

The personnel in IRD and the military services that we interviewed expressed concerns about the qualifications of IRD intake personnel. Specifically, lack of experience among IRD intake staff with the EEO formal complaint process and lack of knowledge regarding the characteristics of EEO complaint cases and documentation needed for these cases were suggested as contributing to delays in EEO complaint processing. To address this, we recommend that the IRD either employ experienced investigators for the intake of requests for investigation or provide more training to IRD staff employed to receive requests for investigation. Budget restrictions may hinder employment of more experienced personnel. Whether or not more experienced personnel can be hired in the near future, increased training should be a priority. Notably, there may be variation in the timeliness of individual IRD personnel, and identifying best practices from the top performers in different positions (e.g., intake, investigators, etc.) may assist with training.

Systematically Implement and Evaluate the Effects of Changes to Complaint Processing Procedures

DoD should systematically implement and evaluate any potential changes that it makes in complaint processing procedures. This will facilitate assessment of the effects that these changes have. The most scientifically rigorous way to do this is with an RCT. An RCT is a study design that involves random assignment of entities into either a group that receives an intervention (i.e., a treatment group), which may involve implementing a change in EEO complaint processing, or a group that does not receive the intervention (i.e., a control group), which may involve continuing to use the current steps and measures to process EEO cases. After study implementation, differences between these groups in terms of the outcomes of interest, such as complaint processing timeliness, may be attributed to the differences in treatment between the groups.

We recommend that an RCT be conducted to assess the effectiveness of checklists in improving accountability and standardization in data and document submission, and thereby reducing complaint processing times. We describe in depth the design of such a study in the main body of the report.

Acknowledgments

The authors wish to thank Clarence Johnson, director of ODMEO, Beatrice Bernfeld, director of Equal Employment Opportunity EEO in ODMEO, and Christopher Brown, director of the IRD of the Civilian Personnel Policy/Defense Civilian Personnel Advisory Service, for their input on this project. We would also like to thank the EEO directors and personnel who provided information to us and participated in discussions with us. In addition, we thank Sean Robson, Louis Mariano, and Abigail Haddad for their comments on earlier drafts of this report.

Abbreviations

ADR	alternative dispute resolution
AFCARO	Air Force Civilian Appellate Review Office
Air Force	U.S. Department of the Air Force
AJ	administrative judge
Army	U.S. Department of the Army
CFR	Code of Federal Regulations and Procedures
DCMO	Deputy Chief Management Officer
DFAS	Defense Finance Accounting Service
DoD	U.S. Department of Defense
EEO	Equal Employment Opportunity
EEOC	Equal Employment Opportunity Commission
FAD	Final Agency Decision
FY	fiscal year
HR	human resources
IRD	Investigations and Resolutions Division
LSS	Lean Six Sigma
MD	management directive

Navy	U.S. Department of the Navy
ODMEO	Office of Diversity Management and Equal Opportunity
OFO	Office of Federal Operations
RCT	randomized control trial
RIE	Rapid Improvement Event
ROI	Report of Investigation

CHAPTER ONE

Introduction

The U.S. Department of Defense (DoD) employs approximately 800,000 full-time civilian employees.[1] Federal laws and executive orders stipulate that it is illegal to discriminate against these persons on the basis of several protected categories.[2] The Offices of Diversity Management and Equal Opportunity (ODMEO) and Civilian Personnel Policy aim to ensure that DoD abides by these laws and orders, thereby allowing DoD civilian employees to work in an environment that is free from discrimination.

If a DoD civilian employee perceives that he or she has been discriminated against, the employee can contact the local Equal Employment Opportunity (EEO) office to discuss the discrimination experience(s).[3] The office will explore potential avenues that may help to resolve the issues raised. If the complaint cannot be immediately resolved, the individual may subsequently file a formal EEO complaint in DoD. Approximately 2,500 to 3,000 DoD civilian employees file formal complaints each year.

---

[1] U.S. Government Accountability Office, *Human Capital: Additional Steps Needed to Help Determine the Right Size and Composition of DoD's Total Workforce*, Washington, D.C., 2013.

[2] See, for example, Title VII of the Civil Rights Act of 1964 (Title VII) and the Pregnancy Discrimination Act amendment to Title VII, the Equal Pay Act of 1963, the Age Discrimination in Employment Act of 1967, Title I of the Americans with Disabilities Act of 1990, Sections 102 and 103 of the Civil Rights Act of 1991, Sections 501 and 505 of the Rehabilitation Act of 1973, and the Genetic Information Nondiscrimination Act of 2008.

[3] EEO is a structure within DoD that exists to ensure compliance with federal nondiscrimination regulations for civilian workforces.

After formal filing, an individual's complaint will go through a multi-step process that, barring the presence of certain exceptions, must be completed within 180 days. In DoD, this process typically involves a transfer of the case file from an agency's EEO office to the Investigations and Resolutions Division (IRD), a directorate within the Civilian Personnel Policy/Defense Civilian Personnel Advisory Service that investigates and mediates complaints for DoD. IRD then transfers the case file back to the appropriate agency EEO office. Since at least 2005, 38 percent to 53 percent of EEO complaints filed each year in DoD have not been processed within the 180-day time frame. When complaint processing (i.e., the time of formal filing to the time an EEO office mails the report of investigation to the person who filed the complaint) exceeds 180 days, not only is DoD in violation of federal regulations, but the employee who filed the complaint may remain in a discriminatory work environment.

In an effort to address delay in formal EEO complaint processing, DoD has participated in program processing evaluations. However, evidence that these evaluations contributed to changes in processing characteristics or improvements in processing timeliness is sparse. Thus, DoD continues to seek out potential causes of this problem and options for improving the timeliness of formal EEO complaint processing.

Purpose of This Report

The purpose of this report is to provide a description of the results of EEO complaint trend analyses, describe findings regarding the potential causes of lag in complaint processing, and outline ways to improve the timeliness of formal EEO complaints in DoD. In addition, we describe in depth the steps DoD can take to implement a randomized control trial (RCT), which can be used to systematically evaluate the effects of changes DoD may make to its complaint processing procedures.

Research Approach

To better understand current formal EEO complaint processing in DoD, we held discussions with EEO directors in DoD agencies and directors in IRD, and we reviewed the documentation they identified as guiding this process. We also obtained and analyzed data from administrative databases in order to examine the trends in formal EEO complaints across DoD and other federal agencies. Further, we analyzed case history data maintained by IRD in order to identify the case characteristics associated with untimeliness. In determining ways to improve complaint processing timeliness, we obtained documentation of previous research on DoD EEO complaint processing and conducted additional discussions with EEO directors. We also conducted discussions of policy and practice with additional key personnel involved in the processing of complaints. Building from these analyses and discussions, we identified four avenues that DoD should pursue to improve the timeliness of the EEO complaint process.

Limitations

This research does not include assessment of the results obtained from a systematic evaluation of a change to formal EEO complaint processing in DoD. As discussed later, additional changes are being made to elements of DoD's formal EEO complaint processing. Thus, implementation of a systematic evaluation during the allowable time frame of this research effort was not possible. As a result, the extent to which each of the changes recommended in this report will actually affect processing timeliness is not known. Further, there is limited available evidence that the recommendations of previous evaluations were implemented by DoD agencies. Agencies within DoD may similarly choose not to institute or systematically track implementation of the recommendations provided in this report.

Organization of This Report

Chapter Two provides a detailed description of EEO discrimination complaint processing within DoD and the military services. Chapter Three provides an overview of a prior evaluation of civilian EEO complaint processing within DoD and its components. Chapter Four presents quantitative data on DoD complaint processing, drawing on EEOC annual reports and IRD's formal EEO complaint case tracking system. Chapter Five presents the findings from our interviews with IRD personnel, and Chapter Six presents findings from our interviews with EEO directors of the military services and personnel at EEO field offices for the services. Chapter Seven describes the design of an RCT that could potentially be used to evaluate whether changes that are made to the EEO formal complaint process in DoD are effective. Finally, Chapter Eight presents our recommendations for improving the timely processing of formal EEO complaints in DoD. An appendix, available separately online at http://www.rand.org/pubs/research_reports/RR680, also provides supporting material that may assist with the implementation of one of our recommendations.

CHAPTER TWO

Equal Employment Opportunity Discrimination Complaint Processing Within the Department of Defense and the Military Services

This chapter summarizes DoD's civilian discrimination complaint process.[1] In addition to considering the general civilian EEO complaint process, we also address how this process is implemented within the specific military services of DoD, focusing on the U.S. Department of the Air Force (Air Force), U.S. Department of the Army (Army), and U.S. Department of the Navy (Navy).

Overview of the U.S. Equal Employment Opportunity Commission

U.S. federal laws outline the illegality of discriminating against a job applicant or employee as based on certain characteristics of that individual.[2] These characteristics include a job applicant's or employee's

---

[1] There is a separate Military Equal Opportunity (MEO) process for addressing discrimination complaints among noncivilians in DoD's military services. Addressing the MEO process is beyond the scope of this report. In addition, this report focuses on individual civilian discrimination complaints, but discrimination complaints may also involve class actions and mixed case complaints, which may be appealed to the Merit Systems Protection Board. For more information on these forms of civilian discrimination complaints, see Title 29 of the Code of Federal Regulations and Procedures (CFR), Part 1614.

[2] Federal laws that are enforced by the U.S. Equal Employment Opportunity Commission (EEOC) include the following: Title VII of the Civil Rights Act of 1964 (Title VII) and the Pregnancy Discrimination Act amendment to Title VII, the Equal Pay Act of 1963, the Age Discrimination in Employment Act of 1967, Title I of the Americans with Disabilities Act of 1990, Sections 102 and 103 of the Civil Rights Act of 1991, Sections 501 and 505 of the Rehabilitation Act of 1973, and the Genetic Information Nondiscrimination Act of 2008.

race, color, religion, sex, age, national origin, and disability. The EEOC coordinates the federal government's nondiscrimination efforts and enforces federal nondiscrimination laws among applicable employers, labor unions, and employment agencies.[3]

To do so, the EEOC must perform several tasks. For example, it uses outreach and training to prevent discrimination, investigates discrimination complaints, and works to fairly address these complaints when it is determined that discrimination occurred. Further, the EEOC works with federal agencies, including DoD, to ensure that they comply with EEOC regulations; assists these agencies with complaint decisions; provides aid to administrative judges (AJs) on EEO complaint hearings; and addresses appeals to federal agency EEO complaint decisions.[4]

EEO Complaint Processing Procedures

The processes and regulations for filing and adjudicating discrimination complaints are listed in Title 29 of the CFR, Part 1614. Part 1614 is well known and well used by EEO program personnel in DoD.[5] In addition, the EEOC disseminates the Equal Employment Opportunity Management Directive (MD)-110 (EEOC, 1999), which gives detailed descriptions of the policies and procedures outlined in Part 1614. It also issues MD-715 (EEOC, 2003), which provides guidance regarding establishing and maintaining an EEO program.

Within DoD, the military services have also created additional documents that address Equal Opportunity (EO) topics, and sections within these documents pertain to the EEO program or complaint

---

[3]   Executive Order 12067 addresses the EEOC responsibility to coordinate the U.S. government's nondiscrimination work.

[4]   EEOC regulations and procedures are described in Title 29 of the CFR, parts 1600 through 1699.

[5]   Information regarding the key documents used by EEO program personnel was obtained from interviews with EEO program leadership in the Air Force, Army, and Navy.

process for the specific service producing the material.[6] For example, Air Force Instruction (AFI) 36-2706 contains sections on the EEO complaint process, as does Army Regulation 690-600. Subchapters within the Navy's Civilian Human Resources Manual address the Navy's EEO program, and the Department of Navy Discrimination Complaints Management Manual discusses the EEO complaint process. Each of these documents provides military service–specific guidance for addressing civilian discrimination complaints within that service, which builds from the EEO regulations for all federal agencies.

There are several steps involved in the EEO complaint process through which DoD civilian employees or applicants must proceed when filing discrimination complaints. Different units or installations within each service have produced multiple flow charts addressing the steps in this process, as described by the EEOC. These charts present similar information in very different ways, and the multitude of EEOC complaint flow charts within and between services has the potential to contribute to confusion regarding the complaint process. Figures 2.1 and 2.2 provide example flow charts that summarize the EEO process within DoD, building from 29 CFR Part 1614, and include the ideal time limits for each stage of the process.[7] Figure 2.1 represents the informal complaint processing procedure; Figure 2.2 shows the formal complaint process, which takes place if a formal complaint is filed.

Informal Complaint Processing
For the complaint to be processed by a DoD EEO office, a civilian who believes he or she has been discriminated against, as based on one or more of the characteristics described in the federal nondiscrimination laws that are covered by the EEOC, must contact the local EEO office

---

[6] EO encompasses principles regarding the treatment of individuals, both generally and in an employment context. EEO is a structure within DoD that exists to ensure compliance with federal nondiscrimination regulations for civilian workforces.

[7] All time periods reference calendar days, such that weekends and holidays are included in the time periods. These figures were modified from an EEO complaint process chart produced by the U.S. Department of the Navy's Submarine Force U.S. Pacific Fleet and a chart used by Marine Corps Camp LeJeune.

Figure 2.1
Informal Complaint Processing

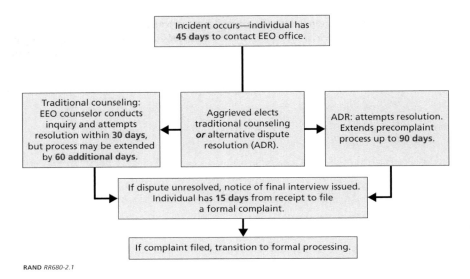

within 45 days of the alleged action or date of action.[8] For the military services, this office may be on or near a military base at which the individual is working or to which he or she has applied to work. When the office has been contacted to make a discrimination complaint, an EEO counselor will inform the aggrieved of his or her rights and responsibilities, obtain contact information for the aggrieved, seek information regarding the complaint, and may offer the option of ADR, which is described in more depth later.[9]

After making the complaint, the aggrieved has the option of either participating in traditional counseling or, if it is offered, volunteering to participate in ADR. If the aggrieved participates in traditional counseling and the complaint is not resolved by this coun-

---

[8]   As described in 29 CFR Part 1614, this 45-day time limit may be extended under some circumstances.

[9]   Section 1614.603 of 29 CFR Part 1614 stipulates that efforts to voluntarily settle complaints will not be made only during informal complaint processing. Rather, efforts will be made throughout the administrative processing of a complaint.

Figure 2.2
Formal Complaint Processing

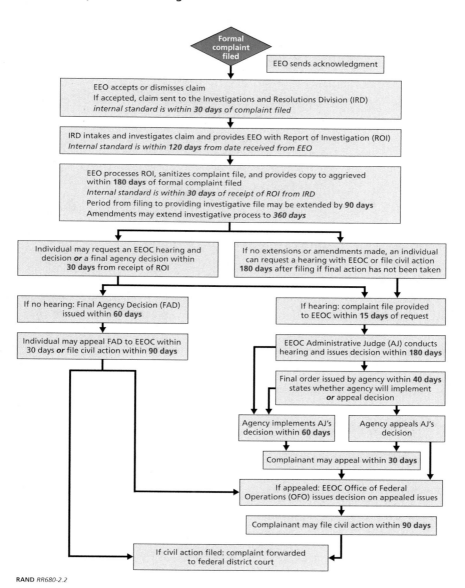

Formal complaint filed

EEO sends acknowledgment

EEO accepts or dismisses claim
If accepted, claim sent to the Investigations and Resolutions Division (IRD)
internal standard is within 30 days of complaint filed

IRD intakes and investigates claim and provides EEO with Report of Investigation (ROI)
Internal standard is within 120 days from date received from EEO

EEO processes ROI, sanitizes complaint file, and provides copy to aggrieved within **180 days** of formal complaint filed
Internal standard is within 30 days of receipt of ROI from IRD
Period from filing to providing investigative file may be extended by **90 days**
Amendments may extend investigative process to *360 days*

Individual may request an EEOC hearing and decision *or* a final agency decision within **30 days** from receipt of ROI

If no extensions or amendments made, an individual can request a hearing with EEOC or file civil action **180 days** after filing if final action has not been taken

If no hearing: Final Agency Decision (FAD) issued within **60 days**

If hearing: complaint file provided to EEOC within **15 days** of request

Individual may appeal FAD to EEOC within 30 days *or* file civil action within **90 days**

EEOC Administrative Judge (AJ) conducts hearing and issues decision within **180 days**

Final order issued by agency within **40 days** states whether agency will implement *or* appeal decision

Agency implements AJ's decision within **60 days**

Agency appeals AJ's decision

Complainant may appeal within **30 days**

If appealed: EEOC Office of Federal Operations (OFO) issues decision on appealed issues

Complainant may file civil action within **90 days**

If civil action filed: complaint forwarded to federal district court seling, the EEO counselor will conduct a final interview with the aggrieved and provide a notice that indicates failure to resolve the complaint within 30 days of the aggrieved contacting the military service's local EEO office. During this 30-day period, the counselor will conduct an inquiry and attempt to find a resolution to the complaint. The specific resolutions offered vary on a case-by-case basis. Before the end of the 30-day period that begins with the aggrieved making the complaint and ends with the final interview, the aggrieved may approve an extension of the traditional counseling process and postpone the final interview by up to 60 days.

The agency decides whether to offer ADR to the aggrieved, and an offer of ADR demonstrates the agency's willingness to participate in the process. If the aggrieved elects to participate in ADR, the time from the date of contact regarding the complaint to the final precomplaint interview and notice can be up to 90 days.[10] ADR can involve a number of different techniques, including mediation, use of an ombudsman, peer review, fact finding, early neutral evaluation, a settlement conference, facilitation, or a mini-trial, which are described in the EEOC MD-110. If a resolution is not achieved during ADR, the EEO counselor will conduct a final interview and provide a notice that indicates failure to resolve the complaint.

Either traditional counseling or ADR may resolve the complaint, and, if so, the complaint process will discontinue. If a resolution to the complaint is not achieved, the aggrieved has 15 days from receiving the notice of failure to resolve the complaint and final interview to formally file a complaint.

Formal Complaint Processing

Once the complaint is formally filed, the local EEO office will send an acknowledgment of receipt of the formal filing to the complainant. This notice provides the date on which the complaint was filed, and it

---

[10] Chapter 3 of the EEOC MD-110 describes ADR and its use. Also see the Administrative Dispute Resolution Act of 1996, Title 5, Part 1, Chapter 5, and the Administrative Dispute Resolution Act of 1998, Title 28, Part 3, Chapter 44.

represents a transition from informal complaint processing to formal complaint processing.

After the complaint is formally filed, the local EEO office will decide whether to accept or dismiss the complaint.[11] If the complaint is fully dismissed, the complainant may file an appeal within 30 days of receiving notification of complaint dismissal or may file a civil action within 90 days.[12] If the complaint is accepted, an investigation must be completed within 180 days of the aggrieved formally filing the complaint. This 180-day time limit is regulated by EEOC and is the focus of this report.[13]

DoD internal standards propose that an EEO office should expect to utilize 30 days to process a complaint once it is formally filed. It is during this period that the EEO office will decide whether the claim is to be accepted or dismissed. If accepted, the complaint is submitted by DoD's local EEO office to IRD. Again, the internal standard for DoD is to transfer the file from the local EEO office to IRD within 30 days. However, this standard can be difficult for EEO offices to meet. For example, the local EEO offices of each of the military services often take more than 30 days for the preinvestigative processing of a formal complaint file.[14]

---

[11] As described in 29 CFR Part 1614, the complaint may be dismissed if it describes an issue that is not addressed by EEOC-covered nondiscrimination laws, fails to comply with stipulated time limits, describes a matter that was not discussed with the EEO counselor, is the basis of a pending civil action in which the complainant is a party, is a complaint in which the complainant has elected to pursue a non-EEO process, or is moot. It may also be dismissed if the complainant cannot be located, does not respond to agency requests within 15 days, alleges dissatisfaction with a previously filed discrimination complaint, or has shown a pattern of misuse of the complaint filing process.

[12] If the complaint is partially dismissed and there is a hearing on the accepted claims, an AJ may review the dismissed issues. If there is not a hearing, an FAD may be issued within 60 days.

[13] Title VII requires the employee or applicant to remain in the administrative process for a minimum of 180 days before the individual can file a civil action. Thus, the EEOC 180-day investigation requirement reflects the statutory exhaustion requirement.

[14] Information regarding EEO office processing times within the military services was obtained during meetings and individual interviews with EEO program leadership in the Air Force, Army, and Navy.

Once received by IRD, the complaint file goes through an intake process. IRD may request additional documentation regarding the complaint from the local EEO office at this time, which often occurs when complaint files are submitted to IRD without all necessary documentation. After the IRD intake process, the file is assigned to an IRD investigator. Internal standards within IRD indicate that IRD investigators are to investigate cases within 90 days of assignment. According to internal DoD standards, IRD is expected to process complaints within 120 days of receiving them from an EEO office. As based on IRD's own internal standards, 90 of these 120 days are to be used for investigation, and 30 days are to be used for intake and final processing. The total 120-day time limit can be difficult for IRD to meet.[15] Once the investigative process is complete, IRD then provides an ROI to the EEO office.

Upon receipt of the ROI, the EEO office processes the file and sanitizes it, which involves the removal of personally protected information, personal health information, and classified information (i.e., redaction). After this is completed, the file is provided to the complainant and, if applicable, the complainant's attorney. Internal DoD standards propose that the time from EEO office receipt of the ROI to provision of the file to the complainant be no more than 30 days. The ROI is to be mailed to the complainant within 180 days of the complaint being filed with the EEO office.

Among the military services within DoD, the 180-day postfiling time period that the EEOC allows for the investigative process is internally divided into three periods: Thirty days are to be used by the local EEO office for formal complaint processing (i.e., acknowledging receipt of complaint, evaluating complaint for acceptance or dismissal, and sending a letter of acceptance or dismissal to the complainant), 120 days are to be used by IRD for the investigative process, and 30 days are to be used by the EEO office to process the complaint file and the IRD-provided ROI. However, the EEO offices and IRD can have difficulty completing their requisite tasks during these time periods.

---

[15] Information regarding IRD processing was obtained during meetings with IRD and EEO program leadership in the Air Force, Army, and Navy.

Greater detail regarding the amount of time currently being used by the EEO offices and IRD is provided in Chapter Four.

The total 180-day investigative process may be voluntarily extended by 90 days if both the complainant and the EEO office agree to the extension. Recently, certain military services have frequently been requesting 90-day extensions early in the 180-day investigative period.[16] This allows the EEO program and IRD additional time to process and review the complaint while still allowing the case to be considered "timely" if it exceeds 180 days in processing.

Further, a complainant may make an amendment or series of amendments to a complaint prior to the conclusion of an investigation. The addition of amendments extends the investigative process. When an amendment is made, the investigative process *from the time of the amendment* is 180 days. There is a limitation for this time period extension, such that the investigative process may not extend past 360 days from the original date the complaint was formally filed.

If amendments or extensions are not made and the investigate process extends past 180 days, the complainant may request a hearing. Recently, the EEOC has indicated that all federal agencies, including the military services, must inform complainants if the services believe that they will not be able to meet the 180-day time period, and, when one provides this notification, it must also inform the complainant of his or her right to request a hearing.[17]

After the complainant receives the ROI, he or she may request either an EEO hearing or FAD. This request must be made within 30 days of the complainant receiving the investigative file. If a complainant either requests an FAD or does not provide a response within 30 days of receiving the file, the EEO office will issue an FAD within 60 days of the conclusion of the 30-day response time allowed to the complainant. The complainant may then appeal the FAD within 30 days of its receipt or file a civil action within 90 days of its receipt. If a civil

---

[16] Information regarding use of extensions was obtained during meetings with IRD and EEO program leadership in the Air Force, Army, and Navy.

[17] For more information, see the Fall 2012 Semiannual Regulatory Agenda (77 Federal Register 43498).

action is filed, the complaint file is forwarded to the federal district court.

If the complainant requests a hearing rather than an FAD following receipt of the ROI, a copy of the complainant's file is provided to the EEOC within 15 days of the receipt of the request. Specifically, this file is provided to an EEOC AJ. The AJ has 180 days from receipt of the complainant's file to conduct a hearing and issue a decision regarding the complaint. This time period may be extended if the AJ indicates that good cause exists for an extension.

Following receipt of the EEOC AJ's final order, DoD's EEO program has 40 days to respond to the order. If the program does not issue an order within 40 days, or if it concurs with the EEOC AJ's final order, the order of the AJ becomes final. Unless reconsideration or exception is made by the military service, the EEOC AJ's final order is to be implemented within 60 days of its receipt by the service.

Following either the final order of the military service's EEO program (i.e., the order that is in response to the AJ's final order) or an EEO program's appeal to an AJ's decision, a complainant may issue an appeal within 30 days. If the complainant, the service's EEO program, or both appeal the AJ's decision, the EEOC office will issue a decision on the appeal. Following that decision, the complainant may file a civil action within 90 days, at which point the complaint file is forwarded to the federal district court.

Military Service Variations in Implementation of the EEO Complaint Process

Each of the military services within DoD processes civilian discrimination complaints using EEOC regulations and guidelines. However, there is variation in how the services implement the process. A better understanding of the variations may facilitate identification of effective methods that may be utilized across the military services. Although an exhaustive description of all differences among the military service EEO programs is beyond the scope of this chapter, Table 2.1 provides

Table 2.1
EEO Complaint Process Variations, by Military Service

Process Element	Air Force	Army	Navy
Use of MicroPact's icomplaints software		√	√
When complainant requests ADR, written and signed explanation required if all necessary parties cannot participate			√
Fact-finding conferences preferred during the investigative process		√	
Requests for time extensions of the 180-day investigative process frequently sent to complainants early in the investigative process		√	√
Request-for-hearing form attached to notice of investigation surpassing 180-day time frame	√		
Some utilization of contracted investigators to process complaints		√	√
Centralized processing of ROIs that are received from IRD	√		
Periodic provision of score cards regarding the performance of the EEO offices at major commands			√

a broad summary of areas in which the military services differ in their processing of civilian discrimination complaints.

First, in terms of tracking and managing civilian discrimination complaint cases, the services use different software packages. For example, the Army and Navy both use MicroPact's icomplaints software.[18] By contrast, the Air Force uses EONET-CIV, a computer system/database to standardize EEO forms and ADR processes within the Air Force.[19] Data regarding the influence of software on processing are not available. However, as later noted in Chapter Three, use of outdated or incompatible software may prevent timelier complaint processing.

---

[18] The icomplaints software system is used by many agencies that are under the jurisdiction of the EEOC. A list of icomplaint customers can be found on the MicroPact website, Customers tab.

[19] AFI 36-2706 makes note of the Air Force's use of EONET.

Next, during precomplaint processing, complainants may be offered the option to participate in ADR. Greater use of ADR may reduce the number of formal complaints filed, which may assist in processing the formal complaints that are filed in a timely manner. ADR is a voluntary process. Thus, agencies may choose whether or not to offer ADR, and, if offered ADR, complainants may choose whether or not to participate. Although the process remains voluntary, the Navy requires that relevant parties employed by the Navy provide an explanation when they decline to participate in ADR with the complainant.[20] For example, if a complainant is offered and agrees to participate in ADR but his manager refuses to join, the manager must provide explanation for this refusal. This requirement is unique to the Navy and is used to promote use of ADRs for addressing complaints. Thus, required management participation in ADR involves either participating in the process or providing explanation for refusal to participate. At that point, higher-level management may then participate in the ADR process. Again, the agency has already volunteered to participate in the process by offering ADR to the complainant.

After a complaint proceeds to the formal processing stage, the services differentially prefer fact-finding conferences during the investigative process. These conferences involve formal meetings with all relevant individuals during which a verbatim record, or transcript, of the proceeding is kept. Although all of the services can make use of these conferences, they are the preferred method for investigations within the Army. Consequently, the Army has tended to utilize these conferences with greater frequency than the Air Force and Navy, which tend to use affidavits.[21]

In addition, as noted earlier, the complainant has an option to volunteer to extend the 180-day investigative process once it has begun. He or she may allow the process to be extended by up to 90 days. The Army and Navy have suggested frequent utilization of early request

---

[20] Information regarding Navy ADR processing times was obtained during individual interviews with EEO program leadership in the Navy.

[21] Army Regulation 690-600 notes that the fact-finding conference is the preferred method for Army EEO investigations.

of extension letters within their service EEO programs. Specifically, soon after the formal investigative period begins, their EEO programs write to complainants to request extensions.[22] Use of these requests can assist the military services and IRD in obtaining more time to process complaints while also allowing the cases to be described as processed on time.

If the complainant does not agree to an extension and the military service reaches or surpasses the 180-day investigative time limit, the service must provide the complainant with a notice of the right to a hearing. When providing these letters to complainants, the Air Force also includes the Hearing Request form that complainants must submit when they choose to go to hearing. Although the Army and Navy provide this letter, they do not routinely include a form for hearing requests.[23] Instead, an Army or Navy complainant must either request a copy of the form from his or her EEO office or obtain a copy online.

When a military service is experiencing a backlog of cases that surpass the 180-day investigative time limit, the service may provide funds to hire contractors to complete the investigative process. DoD does not provide these funds. Rather, they are service-specific funds provided to the EEO program within that service. Since fall of 2012, the Navy has increasingly utilized its own investigative contractors to assist in clearing its backlog of EEO complaint cases. The Army has also indicated frequent use of investigative contractors. However, limited available funds have prevented the Air Force from similarly utilizing its own contract investigators.[24]

Further, the extent to which the processing of complaints is centralized varies across services. For example, the processing of ROIs (e.g., redaction) that are received from IRD may be centralized or conducted

---

[22] Information regarding use of extensions was obtained during meetings with EEO program leadership in the Air Force, Army, and Navy.

[23] Information regarding notice-of-right-to-hearing letters was obtained during meetings with EEO program leadership in the Air Force, Army, and Navy.

[24] Information regarding use of extensions was obtained during interviews and meetings with EEO program leadership in the Air Force, Army, and Navy.

within EEO field offices. The Air Force utilizes a centralized process in which the Air Force Civilian Appellate Review Office manages ROIs from the IRD and notices of rights to complainants. However, EEO field offices in the Army and Navy are included in the processing of ROIs.[25] Use of centralized processing can contribute to difficulty in quickly processing ROIs and returning them to complainants within the 30-day time frame provided to the military services following IRD processing.

Each of the military services participates in evaluations of its EEO programs. Part 1614 of 29 CFR requires that federal agencies periodically review and evaluate their EEO efforts. Further, the OFO produces an annual report documenting information regarding both the discrimination complaints received and the ADR activities conducted by federal agency EEO programs. This information is collected through use of EEOC Form 462.[26] Each of the military services periodically completes Form 462, and each receives a report from the OFO regarding its reported performance. In addition to completing EEOC Form 462 and reviewing the OFO report, the Navy also utilizes scorecards to evaluate the efficacy and efficiency of the EEO offices at each of its major commands.[27] These scorecards, which provide grades (e.g., red, yellow, green) that build from data on timeliness of processing and other data reported in EEOC Form 462, are presented at least biennially to the Assistant Secretary of the Navy and senior leadership within the Navy. The Navy has described the benefits of using these scorecards in its EEO program status report.[28] The use of scorecards is unique to the Navy; neither the Army nor the Air Force utilizes this particular system of evaluation.

Additional differences exist across the military services in terms of their EEO program structures. For example, the Air Force MEO

---

[25]   Information regarding centralization was obtained through interviews with EEO program service heads, AFI 36-2706, and Army Regulation 690-600.

[26]   For more information, see EEOC Form 462: *Annual federal equal employment opportunity statistical report of discrimination complaints user's instruction manual.*

[27]   See Department of the Navy, *EEO Program Status Report Fiscal Year (FY) 2012,* 2012.

[28]   See Department of the Navy, 2012.

and EEO programs are combined, so they often share resources, such as EEO counselors. However, this is not done by the other services. Further, the Navy EEO program is embedded in the Navy Human Resource (HR) program. This may provide some benefits, such that the Navy and EEO programs work to structure their processing guidelines to be more complementary than do the Air Force and Army EEO and HR programs.[29] However, the extent to which these differences in broad structures are associated with differences in the processing of complaints has not been established.

Summary

The EEOC enforces federal nondiscrimination laws and works to ensure that federal agencies, including DoD, fairly and efficiently address individual civilian discrimination complaints. The process that the EEOC has established for agencies to address these complaints contains multiple steps within both precomplaint processing (i.e., before the individual has formally filed a complaint) and formal processing. The EEOC has also established time limits for the steps of the complaint process, and it has been difficult for DoD and its components, which include the Air Force, Army, Navy, and IRD, to meet these time limits.

As part of their own efforts to efficiently and effectively address civilian discrimination complaints, the Air Force, Army, and Navy utilize somewhat different resources or techniques. Despite the variations across services, each of the differentially utilized resources and techniques falls within the guidelines and regulations stipulated by the EEOC for the processing of EEO complaints.

---

[29] Information regarding EEO program resource sharing was obtained during interviews with EEO officers in the Air Force, Army, and Navy.

CHAPTER THREE

Department of Defense's Lean Six Sigma Evaluation of Discrimination Complaint Processing

In an effort to understand and improve its own efforts in addressing the EEOC's regulations and procedures, DoD facilitated a Lean Six Sigma (LSS) evaluation of civilian EEO complaint processing within its components. Conducted during fiscal year (FY) 2012, this evaluation included separate assessments of EEO complaint processing within the Air Force, Army, Navy, and the Civilian Personnel Policy/Defense Civilian Personnel Advisory Service's IRD.[1] A DoD-wide assessment was also conducted following the separate assessments with the different entities. This chapter provides a summary of the LSS evaluation, noting similarities that arose across DoD's components.

LSS Evaluation Process

LSS is a method utilized by DoD to improve the efficiency of its operations. Specifically, Lean is a process that focuses on identifying and discontinuing activities that do not add value to a particular process, and Six Sigma is a data-driven methodology that aims to minimize and control process variation.[2] From March to July 2012, the LSS method was utilized to assess EEO complaint processing within DoD. A primary goal of the LSS evaluation was to determine how to reduce the

---

[1]   An assessment was also conducted on the Defense Finance Accounting Service (DFAS).

[2]   For more information on LSS, see DoD Instruction 5010.43.

time taken by DoD's components (e.g., Air Force, Army, Navy, and IRD) to assess EEO complaints.

Purpose of the LSS Evaluation

The LSS method was implemented to address the amount of time that DoD's components were requiring to process EEO complaints. Although the EEOC allows only 180 days for the investigation of discrimination complaints, the average amount of time that was being used by DoD to investigate these complaints was consistently surpassing 180 days.

Figure 3.1 provides a summary of the overall time the military services reported using to process formal EEO complaints at the time of the LSS.[3] The bars in this figure combine the time used by the IRD to investigate cases and that used by the military services before and after investigation. As of spring of 2012, the military services were exceeding the 180-day regulated time frame for processing.[4]

Implementation of the LSS Evaluation

To conduct the LSS evaluation of DoD's EEO complaint processing, two- to three-day meetings, called rapid improvement events or RIEs, were held with each of the military service EEO programs and the IRD during the spring of 2012. An enterprise-wide meeting was also held, and the military services and IRD jointly participated in this meeting. Attendees at the meetings included facilitators from the Deputy Chief Management Officer (DCMO), experts on the EEO complaint process within the military service, experts on the EEO complaint process within the IRD, and representatives from the Office of the Deputy Assistant Secretary of Defense for Equal Opportunity. Following the meetings, each component of DoD created a report of the findings and

---

[3] The Rapid Improvement Event (RIE) reports provided only averages, which do not permit assessment of variability. Notably, several cases much older than most other cases may increase the observed average processing time. Chapter Four provides additional information regarding the proportion of complaints completed on time.

[4] Information regarding formal processing was obtained from each military service's report on its RIE.

Figure 3.1
Average Formal Complaint Processing Times Reported in the 2012 Rapid Improvement Event Reports

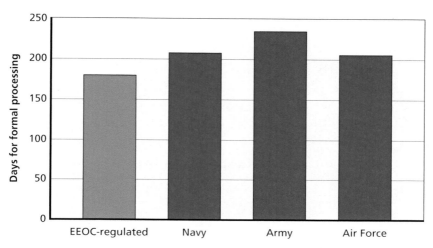

RAND RR680-3.1

recommendations that arose during its meeting. Together, the meeting reports formed the LSS evaluation.

The stated goals for the meetings were to determine the root causes of inefficiencies in EEO complaint processing and to develop solutions to these causes. To address these goals, a multi-step evaluation process was conducted during the meetings. All EEO complaint activities that required DoD resources, more generally, or DoD component-specific resources, more specifically, were identified, and each activity was assessed to determine the extent to which it inhibited effectiveness and efficiency, contributed to processing errors, served as a root cause of error, and contributed to EEO-related work volume without contributing value.

Results of the LSS Evaluation

The RIE findings are summarized in the subsections following, and Table 3.1 provides a summary of the issues raised by the military services during the LSS.

Air Force

The Air Force's RIE was conducted from March 13 to March 15, 2012, and participants included Air Force EEO specialists, managers, and directors; IRD investigators, supervisors, and directors; and DCMO personnel who facilitated the event. In its report, the Air Force

Table 3.1
Summary of EEO Complaint Processing Issues Raised by Military Services

Processing Issue	Air Force	Army	Navy
EEO counselors not recording or framing complaints correctly	√	√	√
Mentoring or training not available for EEO counselors	√	√	√
Lack of accountability for EEO complaint processing performance		√	√
IRD and EEO not providing effective feedback to one another	√	√	√
Community of practice (e.g., shared best practices) does not exist among military services or IRD		√	√
Need for greater standardization of forms and complaint processing	√	√	√
Outdated, incompatible, or unavailable software preventing better complaint processing	√	√	√
Meetings with complainants not being scheduled appropriately	√		
Complainants and managers resisting use of ADR	√		
Deployed civilians not certain whom to contact about complaints		√	
Complainant indecision and late responses reduce timeliness			√
Limited funding for mediators			√

indicated that it was using an average of 208 days to complete the EEO formal complaint process, rather than the EEOC-regulated 180 days.[5] The report noted several issues that may have contributed to the extended EEO complaint processing time. Many of the noted issues concerned EEO counselor activities. For example, RIE participants observed that the Air Force's EEO counselors varied in their ability to record EEO complaints appropriately and were not consistently or correctly framing EEO complaints. Those who attended the Air Force RIE suggested that, when EEO counselors did not frame complaints effectively, this hindered the success of the overall process. However, mentoring and technique training were not available to facilitate improvements in the abilities of the Air Force's EEO counselors, and the online training options that were available for the counselors did not increase desired behaviors.

Limited standardization of forms and processes was also cited as contributing to poor processing. It was noted that, in part due to a lack of standardization, EEO counselors were required to spend the majority of their time performing activities that were not directly related to the processing of EEO complaints, including attending meetings and processing general reports for management, command, or other entities.

In addition, issues in interactions with complainants were raised during the Air Force's RIE. Attendees noted that meetings regarding complaints were not being arranged appropriately by the Air Force EEO local offices. When meetings were scheduled but complainants did not attend the meetings, complainants were not being contacted to reschedule. When complainants and EEO counselors were able to meet, EEO counselors found that both complainants and managers resisted the use of ADR.

Issues regarding working relationships between Air Force EEO counselors and DoD investigators (i.e., IRD investigators) were also raised. Specifically, a lack of transparency was noted, such that EEO counselors and DoD investigators were described as not providing effec-

---

[5]   All information regarding the LSS evaluation of the Air Force was obtained from an internal Air Force report on the RIE.

tive feedback to one another regarding the cause of problems during the EEO complaint process. It was also noted that the responsibilities and requirements of the EEO program personnel and DoD investigators were not well known or clearly defined. Further, a lack of integration between the Air Force's case management system and the system used by IRD was described as contributing to reductions in timeliness.

RIE Recommendations

In an effort to manage the issues that were raised, several recommendations were made during the Air Force's RIE. To address processing issues among EEO counselors, it was recommended that they receive technique training and that claim-writing methods be standardized. To address scheduling issues between EEO offices and complainants, it was recommended that scheduling become a mandatory component of the EEO complaint process. To reduce the disinclination among complainants and managers to utilize ADR, improvements in educating individuals about ADR were recommended. Additional incentives for participating in ADR and performance of reality testing to help complainants fully understand potential outcomes of the complaint process were also suggested. To improve interactions between EEO counselors and DoD investigators, it was recommended that IRD improve awareness and utilization of its website, establish a common user interface for EEO programs, reduce the complexity of its intake process, and improve awareness of the EEO/IRD process.

Army

Participants in the Army's RIE included Army EEO specialists, managers, and directors; IRD investigators, supervisors, and directors; and DCMO personnel who facilitated the event. In its own RIE, conducted from May 8 to May 10, 2012, the Army noted that it was using 235 days to complete the formal EEO complaint investigation process.[6]

Several similarities exist between the Air Force and Army in terms of the issues reported during the RIEs. As the Air Force did, the Army

---

[6] All information regarding the LSS evaluation of the Army was obtained from an internal Army report on the RIE.

noted several issues that arose from the behaviors of its EEO counsel-ors. For example, the Army's EEO counselors were described as fram-ing discrimination complaints incorrectly, and a lack of education for Army EEO counselors was noted as contributing to incorrect reports and actions. However, unlike the Air Force's RIE, the Army RIE spe-cifically noted a general lack of discipline and accountability among the service's counselors. A lack of consequences for poor performance was offered as an additional issue that further exacerbated problems with Army EEO counselor behaviors. In addition, Army commanders were described as unaware of EEO policies and unable to manage EEO counselors effectively.

Similarly to the Air Force, the Army noted issues in correspon-dence between its EEO offices and DoD investigators. For example, it was noted that the complaint tracking system utilized by the Army did not correspond with the system used by IRD, and poor commu-nication between the Army's EEO program, IRD investigators, the Army legal team, and the Army's HR staff contributed to difficulty in processing EEO complaints in a timely manner. In addition, lack of standardization in the EEO complaint process, such as the need for common event codes between IRD and the Army, was also mentioned in the Army's RIE. However, unlike the Air Force's RIE, the Army RIE emphasized that a lack of shared information between IRD and the military services regarding best practices prevented faster improve-ment in complaint processing times.[7]

The Army's RIE also noted that issues arose during the EEO formal complaint process because the Army lacked a digital docu-ment management system, and the Army uniquely commented that deployed civilians were not certain about whom they should contact regarding EEO complaints within the Army.

RIE Recommendations
The Army's RIE recommendations for how to address these issues included implementation of EEO counselor mentoring, certification

---

[7] The Air Force RIE did list best practices as a potential tool for improving counselor education.

of revisions to EEO complaints, and greater reinforcement of EEO policies. To address correspondence issues between the Army EEO and DoD's IRD, the RIE recommended establishing forums of communication for the military services and IRD, encouraging the sharing of best practices of behavior between the services and IRD, and developing digital systems and common event codes that allow for greater integration of complaint tracking between IRD and the Army. In terms of issues that the Army uniquely raised, it was recommended that the Army obtain its own digital document management system and that it develop and disseminate policies regarding deployed civilians.

Navy

The Navy's RIE was conducted from April 17 to April 19, 2012, and participants included Navy EEO specialists, managers, and directors; IRD investigators, supervisors, and directors; and DCMO facilitators. In its final RIE report, the Navy EEO reported an average formal complaint investigation time of 206 days and an unassigned case inventory of 460 cases that were waiting to be investigated for over 60 days.[8] Like the Army and Air Force did, the Navy attributed part of its lack of formal investigation timeliness to the poor performance of EEO counselors, noting that they documented complaints poorly. Similarly to the other services, the Navy also remarked that a lack of training and absence of mentoring contributed to poor EEO counselor behaviors and subsequent lack of timeliness. The Navy also observed that poor supervision, limited accountability, and noncompliance with EEOC regulations were additional factors that contributed to poor EEO counselor behaviors.

In addition, participants in the Navy RIE commented on the difficulty in effectively communicating with complainants, such that indecision and late responses from complainants reduced the timeliness of the Navy's EEO complaint process. Further, limited funding for mediators to facilitate the ADR process and outdated technology and equipment for complaint processing within the Navy EEO were

---

[8]   All information regarding the LSS evaluation of the Navy was obtained from an internal Navy report on the RIE.

also cited as contributing to the service's lack of complaint processing timeliness.

RIE Recommendations

Several recommendations to improve EEO counselor behaviors were listed in the Navy's RIE: the provision of training on how to frame claims, the training of managers and supervisors regarding their responsibilities, quarterly evaluations of the Navy's performance during the EEO complaint process, and regular on-the-job training to ensure compliance with EEOC procedures.

Although IRD was not explicitly named in the Navy's report of key issues within its EEO complaint process, general issues in communication were raised, and the recommendations for improvement in communication included revisions to communication with IRD. To improve communication and collaboration, the Navy RIE recommended establishing a community of practice, developing a directory of EEO practitioners, increased troubleshooting of ongoing issues, and increased correspondence with IRD.

Finally, the Navy provided several recommendations for improving its own program management. These included templates for every aspect of the EEO complaint process that requires correspondence with complainants, development of a manual that outlines complaint procedures, development of guides for how to use different programs and follow certain procedures during the complaint process, and utilization of performance standards.

IRD

After complaints are formally filed with and initially processed by the military services, they are sent to IRD for investigation.[9] As the primary investigative body for EEO complaints in DoD, IRD is a core component of DoD's EEO complaint process. As such, IRD also

---

[9] If cases are dismissed during initial processing, they are not sent to IRD. Further, contract investigators may be used to process cases, and, when this occurs, IRD does not receive the cases.

completed an RIE.[10] Although DoD stipulates that IRD may utilize 120 days to investigate the EEO claims that are received from the military services, IRD reported an average investigation time of 191 days in its own RIE.[11]

Unlike the three-day meetings held by the military services, IRD's RIE lasted only two days, from June 19 to June 20, 2012. In addition, attendees at the IRD meeting differed from those who participated in the military service RIEs, such that participants included a DCMO facilitator and IRD directors and specialists. Although representatives employed by IRD participated in the military service RIEs, representatives employed by the military services did not participate in the IRD RIE. Thus, the military services did not provide input during the IRD RIE, but IRD did provide input during the service RIEs.

Unlike the RIEs conducted by the military services, IRD's findings regarding its own performance focused heavily on data modeling and trend analysis, and the data and programming code for these analyses were not readily available for later inspection.[12] For example, the services created process maps, visual representations of the steps taken to process cases and changes that could be made to the current steps taken. Although it was suggested that similar processing maps were also developed during IRD's RIE, IRD provided only one of these maps, the As-Is Process Map, in its final report. The difference in structure was, in part, due to IRD merging its RIE with the management meeting that the component already held periodically. Thus, IRD used a management meeting to conduct its RIE. Further, participants anticipated discussion points that would be raised during the meeting, and

---

[10] All information regarding the LSS evaluation of IRD was obtained from an internal DoD report on the RIE and from interviews with IRD staff.

[11] There is a three-day discrepancy in IRD investigation time in *Investigations and Resolutions Division Equal Employment Opportunity (EEO) Complaints Process: Rapid Improvement Event (RIE) Final Report* (IRD 2012) and the *EEO E2E Complaints Process Project* (Brown and James, 2012).

[12] IRD did not disseminate documentation on the methods used to conduct these analyses, so we cannot comment on their validity.

they attended the meeting with a list of ideas and supporting data to address the anticipated discussion points.

IRD listed fewer issues than the services did in theirs. Using the analytical models developed by IRD, insufficient numbers of investigators, quality leaders, and case assistants were identified as potential reasons for IRD's lengthy investigative processing time.

RIE Recommendations

In its recommendations, IRD proposed a triage approach to addressing backlogged cases, such that less complex cases should be identified and assigned to investigators immediately. IRD also recommended a two-week blitz of backlogged cases, such that multiple on-site investigations or ADRs should be conducted within a reduced investigation time frame. Informed by LSS participant comments but not on quantitative data, IRD also recommended that it provide an executive summary to AJs who request complaint records, and that it obtain additional resources to handle the case capacity and backlog.

Enterprise-Wide

The enterprise-wide RIE was conducted from June 26 to June 28, 2012, after the meetings for the separate DoD components. It included participants from each of the major DoD components, including the Army, Navy, Air Force, IRD, and DFAS, and, like the other RIEs, it was facilitated by the DCMO. Rather than continuing to extensively outline and address issues in processing, the enterprise-wide RIE focused on developing recommendations to improve the timeliness of complaint processing. Multiple recommendations were raised, and key recommendations, as identified in the EEO enterprise-wide report, are summarized in Table 3.2.

As part of enterprise-wide recommendations for the military service EEO programs, it was recommended that the EEO programs utilize training on the EEO complaint process and framing of claims and that they use more-structured investigation requests, including provision of standardized information across agencies and standard documents requested for each issue filed. Further, the military services were encouraged to collect documents for cases during precomplaint pro-

Table 3.2
Summary of Enterprise-Wide Recommendations

Target of Recommendation	Processing Recommendation
Services	Use training on the EEO complaint process
	Use more-structured investigation requests
	Collect documents before formal filing
	Revisit older cases for resolution
IRD	Hold training on the EEO complaint process
	Provide guidance on investigation requests
	Redesign forms used in the complaint process
	Empower investigators
	Provide more summary and dissemination of data
	Provide executive summaries of cases to administrative judges
IRD and services	Triage complaint cases
	Blitz backlogged cases
ODMEO	Require management to participate in ADR
	Implement mandate to make investigations a priority
ODMEO and DoD	Define the proper role of legal counsel

cessing and revisit older cases to determine whether resolutions might be achieved.

Several recommendations for IRD were also proposed during the enterprise-wide RIE. Although the military services were encouraged to have counselor training, it was recommended that IRD be the entity that holds this counselor training. It was also recommended that IRD provide greater guidance regarding the investigation-related requests that it makes and, relatedly, that IRD restructure the forms it uses during the process. IRD investigators were having difficulty ensuring that meetings scheduled with complainants and associated parties were maintained, so it was recommended that IRD empower investigators to take greater control during this process. It was also recommended that IRD summarize and disseminate data with greater frequency and that it provide executive summaries to AJs who request complaint records. Again, the recommendation for use of executive summaries was based on participant comments, not systematically collected quantitative data.

In the recommendations, it was suggested that both the military services and IRD implement a triage approach to address backlogged cases, such that less complex cases should be identified and assigned to investigators immediately. It was also recommended that a two-week blitz of backlogged cases be held, such that multiple on-site investigations or ADRs should be conducted within a reduced investigation time frame.

Finally, recommendations were made to the ODMEO as well. To facilitate ADR, it was recommended that the ODMEO require management to participate in ADR and that it implement a top-down mandate requiring agencies to make investigations a priority. It was also recommended that the ODMEO more clearly define the proper role of legal counsel.

Implementation of LSS Evaluation Recommendations

The military services, IRD, and the ODMEO have not maintained systematic records regarding how the military services or IRD have addressed the LSS recommendations. Interviews and meetings conducted with DoD component staff, including EEO program directors of the military services, suggested that some of the recommendations have been implemented. We note the implemented recommendations below. If recommendations are not described below, there was no indication among interviewees that the LSS recommendations have been addressed.

Military Service Recommendations

In terms of the military service recommendations, the Air Force participated in EEO counselor training in April 2012. Specifically, in April 2012, the IRD component director of the Air Force held claim training with Air Force EEO counselors. In November 2013, the Air Force also held its own claim training session. There is no available evidence that additional training, above and beyond what was being done before the LSS, has been held by the other military services.

The Air Force also recommended greater education and incentives for ADR. Although Air Force EEO personnel indicated that they have consistently been proactive in promoting ADR, there is no indication that the Air Force has implemented additional ADR education and incentives since the LSS. However, during the fall of 2012, IRD provided ADR education to EEO personnel who were located at Fort Gordon, an Army base in Georgia that had been reluctant to utilize ADR. There is no available evidence that subsequent ADR education has been held at other bases or with other military services.

Further, standardization of forms and the complaint process was recommended by all of the military services. In November 2012, the Navy standardized the EEO complaint processing forms that are used throughout the Navy. The Air Force does not have a standardized set of forms; however, as of November 2013, personnel at the Air Force operations center were working with major commands to obtain the various templates in use at different Air Force EEO field offices, with the intention of synthesizing the forms to create one standardized set of templates. There is no available evidence that the Army has standardized its forms, and there is no evidence of efforts to standardize forms across the military services.

The Navy also recommended that it conduct quarterly evaluations of its EEO complaint processing performance. The Navy continues to make use of scorecards that rate the Navy's major commands, which were already in use before the LSS. There is no evidence available to suggest that additional performance evaluations were implemented following the LSS.

IRD Recommendations

To address the recommendations it raised during its own RIE, IRD has been providing executive summaries to AJs. IRD was also provided with 20 additional investigators.[13] IRD now has approximately 90 investigators on staff. However, the impact of hiring new investigators on processing timeliness could not be determined at the time of this study, because IRD personnel noted that the newly hired investigators were still in training. The extent to which the new investigators assist with improving timeliness may be determined only after the new investigators have completed training. Further, the IRD intake director has triaged cases that were identified as easier to process, including cases that specified a limited number of complainant issues. A blitz of cases was also held. To implement the blitz, IRD component directors identified locations for which there were multiple EEO complaints in process. They subsequently worked in collaboration with the EEO office to establish dates for witness- and complaint-related meetings for multiple cases.

Enterprise-Wide Recommendations

As described above, the military services have participated in limited EEO counselor training, and they have made limited use of standardized EEO complaint processing forms. Further, they have worked in collaboration with IRD to triage backlogged cases and to facilitate the blitz of cases.

IRD has also addressed several recommendations raised during the enterprise-wide event. As noted above, IRD has been providing executive summaries to AJs. In addition to the training event held with Air Force EEO counselors, IRD has redesigned forms used in the EEO complaint process. For example, the request-for-information form provided on the IRD's website was adjusted to facilitate more-accurate and more-complete sharing of information between IRD and the mili-

---

[13] IRD also recently received new software, called Integrated Reliability-Centered Maintenance System (IRCMS), to facilitate correspondence between the military service software systems and that used by IRD. However, attainment of this software was planned before the LSS evaluation.

tary services. To address summary and dissemination of data, IRD produces a monthly report that provides information on case backlog and progress. This is provided to DoD components. In addition, IRD provides the components with a monthly report on the status of each component's cases and their anticipated dates of completion. Finally, IRD has encouraged investigators to take greater charge of complainant scheduling.

To address the recommendations made to the ODMEO during the enterprise-wide RIE, a letter was developed by the Office of the Assistant Secretary of Defense for Equal Opportunity and was sent out on March 20, 2013. This letter reemphasized the EEOC- and DoD-regulated timelines for EEO formal complaint processing, encouraged components to train individuals on the EEO complaint process, and requested a continued commitment to ADR. It also noted that managers and supervisors are responsible for participation in the EEO investigation process. However, the letter stopped short of mandating offers of ADR and requiring management participation in ADR. As such, the utility of the letter has been questioned.[14]

Impact of the LSS Evaluation

Periodic blitz reports produced by IRD suggest that utilizing a blitz tactic to process cases is effective in quickly investigating and settling cases.[15] Additional data regarding the effects of changes that have been made to address the concerns raised during the RIEs are not currently available. Specifically, the comprehensive and continuous collection of information regarding how changes have affected timeliness was not recommended during the LSS, and such information is not currently available.

---

[14] Information regarding the perceived utility of this letter was obtained from interviews with EEO program leadership in the Air Force, Army, and Navy.

[15] One example is Christopher Brown, *Investigations and Resolutions Directorate Blitz Report: May 23, 2013*, Investigations and Resolutions Division, 2013; not available to the general public.

Summary

Several common issues were noted during the military service RIEs (see Table 3.1). For example, each of the military services raised concerns regarding the performance of its EEO counselors, and each also noted a lack of training and mentoring for counselors. In addition, concerns regarding communication between the military services and IRD were also frequently mentioned. Further, the need for greater standardization of the EEO complaint process and forms used during the process was discussed in each RIE, and the need for recent software and technology that facilitate both easier EEO complaint tracking and greater collaboration with IRD was also a common theme in the RIEs. A need for greater accountability among counselors and the development of a community of practice in which best practices for EEO complaint counseling could be shared were also noted. In addition to common themes, the military services also raised service-specific concerns regarding processing.

IRD's RIE was designed differently from those held with the military services, and it produced a different quality of results. For example, the length of IRD's RIE and the diversity of staff present at the event differed from those the RIEs held with the military services. Further, the primary recommendation from the IRD's RIE, namely attaining additional resources, was based on data analysis and modeling that were not used by the military services.

After the individual component RIEs, each of the components met in an enterprise-wide RIE that focused primarily on the development of recommendations to address issues in EEO complaint processing timeliness. There is limited available evidence that the recommendations raised during the military service, IRD, or enterprise-wide RIEs have been addressed in a consistent and comprehensive manner. When recommendations have been addressed, there is limited available evidence that the implemented changes have improved EEO complaint processing timeliness.

CHAPTER FOUR

Timeliness and Completeness in Department of Defense Complaint Processing

Two data sources provide detailed information regarding EEO complaint processing within DoD, which includes the Air Force, Army, and Navy. These data sources are the Annual Federal Equal Employment Statistical Reports of Discrimination Complaints, produced annually by the EEOC with data provided by individual federal agencies, and the IRD's own formal EEO complaint case tracking system, called CaseTrac. Assessments of data from these two sources suggest that neither the EEOC-regulated 180-day time frame nor the DoD-specific internal time divisions of this 180-day time frame is being met.

Limited evidence supports the notion that changes in case complexity, including the number and type of issues and bases per case, can explain the differences in processing time from FY 2011 to FY 2012. Cases with more issues and cases with more bases do tend to take longer to process than those with fewer issues and bases. In addition, cases with certain types of issues and those with certain types of bases also take longer to process than those with other types of issues and bases. However, these factors account for little variance in case processing times. Further, there is little evidence of compositional changes in cases (e.g., more cases filed with more of the kinds of issues or bases that take longer to process) from FY 2011 to FY 2012, suggesting that changes in case complexity may not be influencing changes in processing times. Due to the limited available time span of case information, it is more difficult to analyze whether a backlog of unfinished cases drove later delays in case processing times, and we cannot rule this out.

DoD Processing Timeliness

Data from the EEOC annual reports demonstrate that the percentage of EEO formal complaint investigations completed within a timely manner by DoD, defined as within the 180-day time frame that is regulated by the EEOC, has gradually decreased since 2007.[1] To determine whether reduced complaint processing timeliness may be a systemic problem for certain federal organizations, we conducted additional analyses. Specifically, we created a comparison group of similar federal organizations to determine how changes in DoD's percentage of investigations completed on time compared with the percentage of timely investigations within similar organizations. To create this group, we assessed the sum of timely investigations and sum of total investigations from the following organizations: Defense Distribution Center, Defense National Imagery and Mapping Agency, Defense Nuclear Facilities Safety Board, Defense Reutilization and Marketing Service, Defense Supply Center Columbus, Defense Supply Center Philadelphia, Defense Supply Center Richmond, Department of Energy, Department of Homeland Security, Department of State, Department of Veterans Affairs, Drug Enforcement Administration, EEOC, Federal Bureau of Investigation, Federal Labor Relations Authority, Fleet Forces Command, Military Sealift Command, National Credit Union Administration, Office of the Director of National Intelligence, Selective Service System, U.S. Coast Guard, Defense Human Resources Activity, Defense Office of the Secretary–Washington Headquarter Services, and Defense Technical Information Center.[2] As seen in Figure 4.1, the percentage of timely investigations for this comparison group has shown a steady increase from 45 percent in 2006 to 71 percent in 2011. Because comparable agencies are demonstrating an increase in processing timeliness, the decrease in DoD's timeliness does

---

[1]   For the purposes of this report, we operationalize DoD entities as those that utilize IRD to assist in processing complaints.

[2]   Although some of these entities are part of DoD, they were not included as part of the DoD aggregate because they do not utilize IRD to assist in processing complaints.

Figure 4.1
Percentage of Investigations Completed on Time

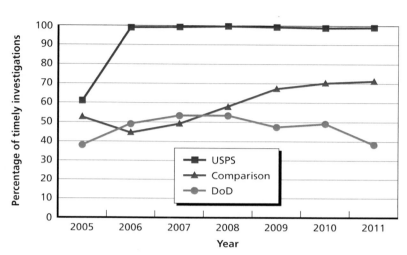

NOTE: USPS = U.S. Postal Service

RAND RR680-4.1

not appear to be due to systemic issues that are affecting similar types of federal agencies.

In addition, USPS is a large U.S. federal agency (i.e., 15,000 employees or more) that consistently reports some of the highest rates of EEO counselings and complaints filed, and it reports some of the highest rates of EEO counselings completed and EEO investigations completed on time. As such, we also assessed it as a comparison agency to DoD. In contrast to DoD, the USPS has completed almost 100 percent of its formal complaint investigations on time since 2006. Again, this suggests that issues in DoD's EEO complaint processing timeliness may be unique to DoD.

To further examine these comparisons, we conducted regression analyses in which we predicted the percentage of investigations with timely completions by agency in terms of both the year of investigation and whether the agency was DoD that used IRD (as opposed to in the comparison group or USPS).[3] As an example of the unit of observation, the Air Force is a DoD agency that provides one observation per year for total number of completed investigations and one observation for total number of investigations completed timely, which can then be used to determine percentage of investigations with timely completions. We used a weighting procedure in which, in order to make agencies' handling of more complaints account for more, each agency was weighted by the number of total completed investigations.[4] Results showed that DoD is significantly less likely to have timely investigations than non-DoD entities are.[5] This result is highly statistically significant and robust to the exclusion of either USPS or the comparison group, although the difference between DoD and USPS in terms of on-time completion rate is significantly larger than the difference

---

[3]   These analyses assess how DoD is performing in comparison to other exemplar agencies with similar backgrounds that are also not meeting the 180-day requirement.

[4]   For weighting, we used the delta method to derive the weight for the weighted least squares estimator (George Casella and Roger L. Berger, *Statistical Inference,* 2nd ed., Boston, Mass.: Cengage Learning, 2001; Douglas C. Montgomery, Elizabeth A. Peck, and G. Geoffrey Vining, *Introduction to Linear Regression Analysis,* 5th ed., Wiley, 2012). This was done to address the composition of the available data. Specifically, weights were calculated as follows:

$$\hat{p} = \text{percentage of investigations timely}$$

$$Y = \log\left(\frac{\hat{p}}{1-\hat{p}}\right)$$

$$\text{var}(\hat{p}) = \frac{\hat{p}(1-\hat{p})}{\text{number of investigations}}$$

$$\text{var}(Y) = \text{var}(\hat{p}) \times \left(\frac{1}{\hat{p}(1-\hat{p})}\right)^2$$

$$w = \frac{1}{\text{var}(Y)}.$$

[5]   Assessments demonstrated that the assumption of homoscedasticity was met, with approximately equal variance across time points.

between DoD and the comparison group.[6] This confirms the impression given by Figure 4.1.

DoD Internal Timeliness

DoD's internal standards for EEO complaint processing stipulate that, once a formal complaint is filed, 30 days may be utilized by the agency (e.g., Air Force, Army, or Navy) to process the formal complaint and that after this initial 30 days, the complaint is to be sent to IRD for investigation. DoD's internal standards also stipulate that IRD is allowed 120 days to investigate the complaint before providing its ROI to the agency. Finally, 30 additional days may be used by the agency to process the ROI before providing it to the complainant. Thus, DoD's 30-120-30–day time division for EEO complaints should meet the EEOC-regulated period of 180 total days for formal processing.

To examine whether DoD was meeting this internal time division, we examined data from IRD's CaseTrac system. Notably, IRD does not collect or maintain data on the final agency processing of ROI.[7] Thus, we did not examine the final 30-day period allotted by DoD for agency processing. Rather, we considered only the first two periods of DoD's internal time frame, namely agency initial processing and IRD investigation. Further, data were made available for cases filed with IRD from October 2010 to September 2012, which permitted assessment of cases filed during a relatively limited time frame. Finally, the analyses excluded cases for which amendments were made, cases with obvious data errors, and cases filed with the initial agency (e.g., Army, Navy, Air Force) before October 2010. This last exclusion crite-

---

[6] Comparable regression analyses comparing DoD entities that do not use IRD with the remainder of the entities in the comparison group showed that these entities were significantly less timely than the other entities in the comparison group. Additional analyses showed that these entities were also significantly less timely than the DoD elements that use IRD. However, the number of completed cases for all non-IRD DoD agencies ranged from 19 to 43 between 2005 and 2011. Thus, these patterns, which involve a limited number of cases from non-IRD DoD elements, should be interpreted with caution.

[7] The EEOC annual reports do not contain information regarding these internal time divisions.

rion was implemented in order to address a limited number of outliers (N = 250) with excessively long initial agency processing times.

Assessment of cases processed during FY 2011 and FY 2012 showed that the initial agency processing time for DoD decreased from an average of 48 days in FY 2011 to an average of 38 days in FY 2012. To determine whether this reduction was due to reductions in the time required by specific agencies, we examined the average initial processing time used by each of the military services during FY 2011 and FY 2012. We saw a similar decrease in the number of days for initial agency processing for the specific agencies of the Air Force, Army, and Navy, although none reached DoD's internal timeliness standard of 30 days for initial agency processing (see Figure 4.2).

Figure 4.2
DoD Internal Processing Times

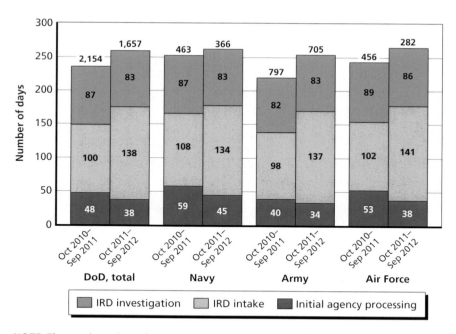

NOTE: The total number of agency cases submitted to the IRD for each fiscal year is shown above each bar.

By contrast, the IRD investigation time used to process DoD cases increased from FY 2011 to FY 2012 (see Figure 4.2). We conducted assessments to determine whether certain periods of IRD processing are contributing to the agency's timeliness issues. When IRD receives a case, the case first goes through an initial intake period. During this time, IRD intake staff members ensure that the case is entered into the IRD's case tracking system, that the files needed to investigate the case have been submitted by the agencies, and that the case is assigned to an investigator. Afterward, an IRD investigator examines the case and produces an ROI for each case he or she is assigned.[8] In effect, IRD has two internal periods within the 120 days that is allocated to investigate cases, namely an intake period and an investigation period.

As seen in Figure 4.2, the average number of days that IRD uses to intake cases increased from FY 2011 to FY 2012. By contrast, the average number of days used to investigate cases decreased. Overall, these data suggest that a lack of timeliness in DoD's EEO complaint processing since October 2010 has been due to increases in the time that cases spend with IRD intake. As discussed in Chapters Five and Six, this may be due to lack of processing timeliness on the part IRD intake personnel or a lack of timeliness by the services in providing the information requested by IRD intake personnel.

DoD Caseload

The decrease in the timeliness of DoD formal complaint investigations may be due, in part, to an increase in the number of precomplaint counselings performed by and the number of formal complaints filed with DoD each year. For example, if a greater number of cases is filed annually, this may strain DoD's resources and decrease the percentage of timely investigations. To examine this possibility, we assessed the number of counselings per employee, percentage of coun-

---

[8] Notably, the IRD investigator may request additional files that were not requested or obtained by IRD intake. However, the time used by the investigator to obtain these files is associated with the IRD investigation time, not the IRD intake time, in the IRD database.

Table 4.1
Summary of Trends in Caseload, 2005–2007

Agency and Characteristic	Fiscal Year						
	2005	2006	2007	2008	2009	2010	2011
DoD							
Counselings per employee	0.010	0.009	0.008	0.008	0.008	0.008	0.009
Complaints per employee	0.005	0.004	0.004	0.004	0.004	0.004	0.004
Total number of counselings	6,317	5,902	5,533	5,485	5,894	6,121	6,873
Total number of complaints	2,893	2,610	2,645	2,743	2,790	2,998	3,437
Comparison							
Counselings per employee	0.014	0.013	0.013	0.012	0.012	0.011	0.011
Complaints per employee	0.007	0.006	0.006	0.006	0.006	0.006	0.006
Total number of counselings	7,101	6,823	6,732	6,871	8,111	7,449	7,389
Total number of complaints	3,315	3,207	3,157	3,438	4,091	3,794	3,800
USPS							
Counselings per employee	0.023	0.021	0.022	0.024	0.024	0.024	0.023
Complaints per employee	0.009	0.008	0.008	0.008	0.008	0.008	0.008
Total number of counselings	18,349	16,954	17,285	18,307	17,079	16,300	14,683
Total number of complaints	6,836	6,040	5,879	5,921	5,400	5,285	4,837

selings ending in complaints per employee, total volume of counselings, and total volume of complaints recorded within the EEOC's annual reports. In addition to examining trends in DoD, we also examined trends associated with USPS and the previously described comparison group.

As shown in Table 4.1, the rate of counselings and complaints per DoD employee did not demonstrate a dramatic increase from FY 2005 to FY 2011, and, in fact, a slight decrease was seen. However, the volume of DoD counselings increased from 6,317 in 2005 to 6,873 in 2011, and the volume of DoD complaints also increased from 2,893 in 2005 to 3,437 in 2011. Overall, this shows that the rate of counselings and complaints filed over time was slower than the rate of DoD increases in employees hired. Similarly, the rate of counselings and complaints for the comparison group of similar federal agencies showed a slight decrease from 2005 to 2011, but, as at DoD, the volume of counselings and complaints for this group also increased. Finally, the number of counselings and number of complaints performed by USPS each year are much greater than the numbers performed by DoD. The rate of counselings and complaints per USPS has remained relatively stable, and the total volume of USPS counselings and complaints decreased from 2005 to 2011.

We conducted additional regression analyses in which we predicted the percentage of timely investigations using the year of investigation, a dichotomized DoD variable, and number of completed precomplaint counselings at the agency level. Again, in order to reflect significant differences in the number of complaints processed by agency, we used the number of completed complaints as a frequency weight. Results showed that the number of completed counselings was not a statistically significant predictor of percentage of investigations completed within 180 days. In other words, more precomplaint counselings is not significantly associated with fewer timely investigations. This suggests that the issue in timely processing does not lie with the number of complaints that agencies are facing.

The DoD comparison group showed similar trends to those for DoD in rate and volume of EEO counselings and complaints. As shown in Figure 4.1, this comparison group has increased its percentage of timely investigations, whereas DoD has decreased its percentage of timely investigations. These trends suggest that the delay in processing within DoD is not due to unique changes in the rate and volume of counselings and complaints occurring within DoD.

DoD Case Complexity: Issues and Bases

In addition to some increase in case volume, the composition of the complaints filed may demonstrate a change. Specifically, the number of cases that are more complex and require a greater amount of time to process may be increasing, even though the overall number of cases is not changing dramatically. To assess this possibility, we examined data from IRD's CaseTrac system to determine which types of cases involve the lengthiest processing times for the initial agencies and IRD. We concluded that these changes are not sufficiently significant to explain the change in processing times; that is, increases in case complexity are not causing major changes in processing times.

Cases may be classified by *bases* or *issues* associated with the cases. *Bases* involve the characteristics of the complainant on which the acts of discrimination are based. For example, a complainant may have been discriminated against because of race, color, sex, religion, national origin, age, disability, or genetic information. By contrast, *issues* involve how the complainant was discriminated against or what acts of discrimination were performed against the complainant. Example issues include discrimination experienced in terms of training opportunities provided, scores received on an examination or test, and awards allocated.

Issues or bases that require more time to process may qualify as being more complex. We analyzed complaints filed from October 2010 and September 2012 to determine which issues or bases require more time to process. We then performed additional analyses to determine whether changes in the number or type of issues and bases could explain overall changes in processing time by period. The consistent finding was that, although there were differences in processing times across period, these could not be explained by changes in case complexity—number of issues or bases or type of issues or bases.

Initial Agency Processing

On average, DoD agencies utilize the most time to initially process cases involving the bases of equal pay for males, equal pay for females, color, religion, and the national origin category of "other." However, the number of cases filed for these bases has not increased since October 2010. This suggests that the decrease in DoD processing timeliness is not due to an increase in the number of cases involving complex bases of discrimination (see Figure 4.3).[9]

Although the number of complex bases has not shown a dramatic increase, the number of complex issues may be increasing and

Figure 4.3
Changes in Number of Cases Filed for Bases with Lengthiest Initial Processing

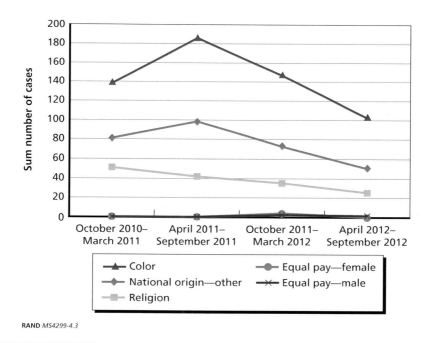

RAND MS4299-4.3

---

[9] In addition, we performed regressions explaining each processing time (initial agency processing time, IRD intake time, and IRD investigation time) both in terms of when a case was filed and in terms of when a case was filed and which bases it involved. We found that adding in bases did not significantly change the coefficients on when the case was filed, meaning that the differences in initial agency processing time could not be explained by changes in which bases cases involved. We did the same with case issues and again found that including case issues did not change the coefficients on time period filed for initial agency processing time, IRD intake time, or IRD investigation time.

subsequently influencing initial EEO formal complaint case processing timeliness within DoD. Therefore, we examined case issues next.
When considering all issues, DoD utilizes the most time, on average,
to initially process the following five issues: examinations, reinstatement, awards, training, and duty hours. Thus, when the amounts of
time used to process cases with different issues are compared, these five
issues spend more time in processing than the other issues that may be
associated with a case. As seen in Figure 4.4, the number of cases filed
with DoD for these issues has not increased since October 2010. Addi-
tionally, we performed regression analysis modeling processing time
in terms of both time period filed and time period filed plus issues.
Time period was segmented into six-month periods.[10] The coefficients
on time period filed did not significantly change with the inclusion of

Figure 4.4
Changes in Number of Cases Filed for Issues with Lengthiest Processing

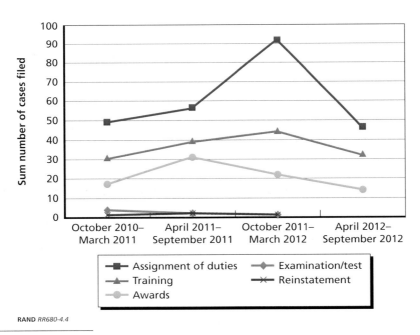

RAND RR680-4.4

[10] Assessments demonstrated that the assumption of homoscedasticity was met, with
approximately equal variance across time points.

issues. This suggests that the decrease in DoD processing timeliness is not due to an increase in the proportion of cases involving complex issues of discrimination.

IRD Processing

We conducted parallel analyses for IRD, assessing the time required by IRD to intake and investigate the different bases and issues. IRD uses the most time to intake cases involving the following bases: genetic information, equal pay for females, physical disability, the racial category of "Asian/Pacific Islander," and mental disability. It uses the most time to investigate cases involving equal pay for males, reprisal, color, the national origin category of "other," and the racial category of "black." Analyses showed that the number of cases involving these bases has not changed significantly since October 2010.

Next, IRD uses the most time to intake cases involving the following issues: conversion to full time, appointment or hire, assignment of duties, reprimands, and training. It uses the most time to investigate cases involving reinstatement, denied reassignment, awards, reasonable accommodation, and nonsexual harassment. Overall, the number of cases involving these issues has also not increased since October 2010.

These analyses suggest that the numbers of cases involving complex issues or bases are not significantly increasing. Specifically, cases involving bases and issues for which the agencies and IRD use more time to process did not generally show increases in FY 2011 or FY 2012. Thus, increases in DoD processing times do not appear to be due to changes in the bases or issues associated with the formal complaints filed.

DoD Case Complexity: Number of Issues

A complainant may file one complaint that lists more than one issue (i.e., more than one way in which discrimination occurred). Cases that list more issues may be considered more complex than cases that list only one issue. Hence, a case with multiple issues filed may take longer to process than a case that has only one issue. To assess this, we used data from IRD's CaseTrac to run a series of three bivariate regression analyses. For these analyses, we entered the number of case issues as the predictor and the length of time in initial processing, length of time in IRD intake, and length of time in IRD investigations served as the variables to be predicted. Although significant, the size of the associations between the number of issues per case and the length of processing time initially used by the agencies was small. As the number of issues per case increased by one standard unit, initial agency processing time increased by only 0.06 of a standard unit (β = 0.06, $p < 0.001$), the length of time in IRD intake time increased by .12 of a unit (β = 0.12, $p < 0.001$), and the length of time in IRD investigations increased by 0.09 of a unit (β = 0.09, $p < 0.001$). These are small increases in processing time in relation to increases in number of issues. Figure 4.5 shows the relationships between number of issues per case and each of the three processing times.

An additional assessment was conducted to assess whether cases filed in FY 2012 contained more issues per case than cases filed in FY

Figure 4.5
Number of Issues per Case and Processing Times

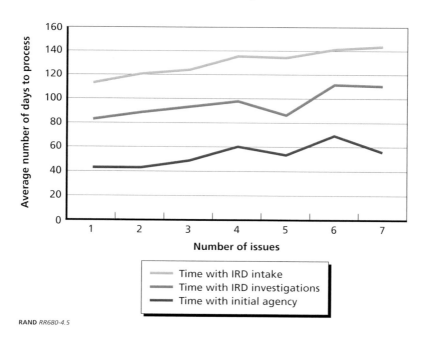

2011. To conduct this analysis, an independent sample t-test was performed. Results showed a significant difference between cases filed in FY 2011 and FY 2012 ($t(3,231.69)$ = 5.29, p < 0.001).[11] There were significantly more issues per DoD case in FY 2012 (M = 1.60, SD = 0.95) than in FY 2011 (M = 1.41, SD = 0.80). This means that cases filed in FY 2011 had an average of 1.41 issues, whereas cases filed in FY 2012 had an average of 1.60 issues.

Although there are overall differences in average processing time by case complexity, differences in case complexity explain only a small amount of the variation in case processing time and therefore are not a likely contributor to changes in processing time from FY 2011 to FY 2012. Differences in complexity, including the number of issues, the number of bases, and every specific issue and basis, explain less than 5 percent of the variation in terms of overall processing time. The explanatory value is even lower when focusing on specific subsets of processing time: initial agency time, IRD intake, and IRD investigation. It is similar when focusing on these processing time subsets for particular agencies. Because of this, and the small compositional changes in case complexity from FY 2011 to FY 2012, we conclude that changes in case complexity are not meaningfully affecting changes in time to case completion.

Summary

Given comparison with other exemplar agencies, DoD's inability to process EEO complaints within the EEOC's regulated time frame does not appear to be due to unique characteristics of DoD. Specifically, number of complaints per employee, counselings per employee, and investigations per employee are not larger for DoD than for the comparison group. Changes in case complexity also do not appear to contribute greatly to untimeliness. Due to the limited time frame of available data, we are unable to evaluate whether changes in overall

---

[11] A Levene's test for equality of variances showed a significant difference between the group variances. As a result, equal variances were not assumed.

caseload have affected timeliness via creating a backlog of unresolved cases. Resource issues, including the number of staff, competency of staff, and quality of technology, may also be related to processing timeliness and case completeness. However, comprehensive and systematically collected data on staff characteristics and training are not currently available.

CHAPTER FIVE

Perceptions of and Potential Avenues for Improving Timeliness of EEO Complaint Processing in IRD

To consider potential avenues for improving the timeliness of EEO complaint processing in DoD, we conducted interviews with IRD personnel. During these interviews, we posed questions regarding the current processing of formal EEO complaints and suggestions for potential improvements that could be made to improve the timeliness of processing. Initial themes arose for avenues to pursue in improving the timeliness of EEO complaint processing. Overall, interviews suggested four potential avenues for improving the timeliness of EEO complaint processing: Two involved ways to address case backlog and reduce the current formal complaint caseload, and two involved adjustments to current complaint processing that may facilitate greater rapidity of processing in DoD.

IRD Perceptions of Processing Timeliness

We conducted interviews with 12 IRD employees to assess their perceptions of EEO formal complaint processing timeliness. To obtain a list of IRD personnel who could be interviewed for this project, we asked the director and deputy director of IRD to provide the names, email addresses, and phone numbers of individuals who each held different job positions within IRD. Further, we asked the director and deputy director to limit the list of individuals to those who would be willing and able to provide their thoughts regarding the current process and potential adjustments that may be made to improve the timeliness of EEO complaints in DoD. Upon receiving a list of individuals, a

RAND researcher emailed the individuals, requesting their participation in a telephone interview and providing a brief description of the project and the topics that would be addressed during the interview. During the fall of 2013, phone interviews were scheduled with those who agreed to participate.

A RAND researcher conducted semistructured interviews with 12 IRD personnel. Each interview lasted approximately 45 to 60 minutes. During each interview, either a graduate student or research assistant recorded notes. All participants were informed that notes would be taken during interviews and that they had the right to refuse to participate or to answer any question. Participants represented eight different types of employment positions in IRD.[1]

We asked the IRD interviewees questions about their perceptions of the speed of formal EEO complaint processing during different periods of the complaint process. Specifically, they were asked which parts of the process move the most slowly and which parts move the most quickly. They were also asked to provide their recommendations for improvements that could be made to increase the timeliness of the process.

Delays in Data and Documentation Submission

Several participants indicated that obtaining data or documentation from the requesting agency, which includes the Air Force, Army, or Navy, took a considerable amount of time. On its website, IRD provides a list of data files and documents needed for formal EEO complaints involving certain bases or issues. IRD has requested that, when it submits a request for investigation, an agency submit the documents listed on this site, because these documents facilitate the investigation process. Agencies and their EEO offices have access to this website and may use it when determining which documents to submit with a par-

---

[1]   Fewer than ten individuals hold several of the IRD employment positions of the personnel that were interviewed, and thus, the title of each interviewee's employment position has been withheld from this report.

ticular case. However, they are not required to submit the listed documents. After an EEO office has collected what are perceived by the office to be the appropriate documents for a case, it submits a request for investigation to IRD with the collected documents. After that, IRD intake personnel review the submitted case and may request documentation listed on the website but missing from the case file.

The slowness of additional documentation submission was a common theme that arose during interviews, and the extent to which the IRD website is used by those who are submitting formal complaints to the IRD for investigation was questioned. For example, one interviewee noted the following:

> The agencies, for whatever reason, are not providing documents up front. It would be quite simple for the EEO offices to read our website and our list of documents and, based on the list, provide all those up-front. Then, we wouldn't have to do a document request except for things that they forgot, and we can eliminate that whole [IRD intake] staff. And the investigators can concentrate on other documents they forgot or [were not] apparently needed until they got into the investigation.

Similarly, one interviewee made the following comment:

> Virtually always, when we get a case for an agency, an intake person—an administrative person—will find [that] the agency did not forward all of the documents that will be necessary for that case. So we have to go back and request documents. This causes further delay. Now, we in IRD have given agencies lists of the types of documents required for types of cases. . . . The agencies know what we're looking for, but [they] routinely fail to provide all of them.

Another interviewee stated,

> Intake gets that case. Documents are missing. First hold-up. They ask for documents. The activity doesn't give it to them. They ask again. They can't hold that case up. The clock is still ticking. They give it to [the] investigator, who has 90 calendar days.

These comments suggest that one area to address in terms of improving the timeliness of EEO complaint processing is data and document submission to IRD.

Recommendations for Improving Data and Documentation Submission

Participants provided their thoughts for improving data and documentation submission. One recommendation was to require, rather than recommend, that agencies provide the documents listed on the IRD website. One interviewee stated,

> But I think if the agencies provided documents up-front when they submitted the case file, then that would be more efficient, and would help the process move more quickly. If they had a stance that we [at IRD] wouldn't accept a case unless they [at the agencies] have all the documents, or most of the documents, then that would be a more efficient process.

In responding to how they would improve the timeliness of EEO processing, another interviewee noted, "I would have an organized case file with all standardized documents, and I would only have to order extraordinary docs."

Another interviewee commented,

> Do it [send the documents] up-front. It's not that complicated. These complaints fall in certain categories. Each category, we ask for the same documents for the same things. How ever many we do a year—there's a pattern here. But it seems like we reinvent the wheel a lot on this.

The recommendations of IRD interviewees suggest that greater accountability for and standardization of data and document submission to IRD may improve the process. One way to accomplish this may be through required use of checklists by the agencies, such that an agency that is submitting a case to IRD must indicate which IRD-needed documents it has submitted. Notably, the IRD website may not be clear regarding what information is needed and may request information that is not needed. Thus, these checklists would need to explain clearly what documentation is needed and should list only documentation that is needed for investigations to address the cases, not documentation that is rarely used. When not submitting documents, an agency submitting a case would need to provide an explanation for document exclusion. When asked about the potential use of checklists to facilitate accountability and standardization, an interviewee noted, "It would definitely help out if they already have this checklist. It has to start with the counselor."

Delays Due to Limited Experience of IRD Intake Personnel

Interviewees also questioned the speed and efficacy of IRD intake personnel. They suggested that IRD intake contributes to delays in EEO formal complaint processing. For example, one interviewee noted, "From what I see, the problem lies with our intake unit."

Participants commented that IRD intake staff members have limited familiarity with formal EEO complaint case processing or with the documentation needed to investigate certain complaint cases. They proposed that this lack of knowledge may contribute to intake staff requesting documentation from the agencies that is not needed, requesting documentation that has already been submitted, and making cases available to investigators despite a lack of essential documentation. One interviewee commented,

> The [intake] reviewers are GS-7 [General Service level 7]. [In the past], they were GS-13s who were previously investigators. The concept of what was needed, being able to quickly recognize what's in the files, what the forms are, what it means—it was easier, versus a GS-7 with no real background in HR or EEO. They came from admin ranks and were reclassified. It just happened.

Interviewees' comments suggest that improvement should be made to address the current inexperience of IRD intake staff.

Recommendations for Improvements to IRD Intake

Interviewees provided several different ways to address delays perceived to be caused by IRD intake personnel. One proposed option was to employ individuals with more experience to review the cases that are submitted to IRD for investigation. An interviewee stated,

> I don't know that [intake] need GS-13s. An 11 at a minimum—somewhat more experienced. . . . It would be more productivity at a higher grade, but I agree they're not a 13.

Another proposed option was to eliminate IRD intake review staff and instead have cases directly assigned to investigators for review. Under this proposal, investigators, rather than intake staff, would organize case files and request additional documentation. One interviewee commented,

> Even in the past, before we had an intake unit, we had the investigator doing the document request—I actually think that is more efficient. . . . An intake [staffer] may not know enough about the case to request the right document, and in addition, it's duplicating work, since it means two people have to look through the file and understand the case and theories and determine which documents are needed—the intake and investigator have to both do it, so the investigator has to review the cases and get witnesses, and they are ultimately responsible for making sure that the docs are there, and if intake forgets it or doesn't realize what documents are needed, then the investigators have to do it, so that is a duplication of work.

However, the transfer of current intake review responsibilities to investigators was not universally supported. One investigator noted,

> When I started at the organization, intake didn't exist—and I think it is the best thing that happened. . . . Intake takes care of the triage of the case—they get the case in hand, and we used to give . . . we used to be assigned a case, and you would have to do everything—you get all these documents in no order, all these documents, and they organize the documents. . . . They don't

do the evidence part of it, but they put it in order and make sure that the former complaint, counselor's report, notice of rights and responsibilities, notice of receipt—these are all everything I need for the case file, so just having that little portion of the entire case file organized, is very helpful.

A third option may be to provide more training to the intake staff who are employed to review the cases submitted to IRD for investigation. When asked how often intake personnel go to training, one interviewee stated, "Not very often." Another stated that the training that intake staff members receive is "not nearly as formal as the training that investigators get." This suggests that the current formal training provided to intake staff may need to be increased.

Delays Due to Case Backlog

Of note, several interviewees commented that IRD had recently received a high number of cases. The receipt of this high number of cases was perceived as contributing to a case backlog at IRD, such that IRD did not have sufficient resources to rapidly process a sudden increase in cases. One interviewee noted, "With IRD's backlog, we got a class complaint. One day, 200 [or] 300 cases. That's definitely going to affect the backlog. Definitely affects processing time. Investigators can only take so many cases." Another interviewee stated, "The slowest step is assignment of cases to investigators, due to a backlog."

These comments suggest that IRD may have difficulty in rapidly processing formal EEO complaint cases when it receives a higher number of cases than average. Interviewees noted that IRD had been able to "chew through the backlog and assign cases earlier." However, the possibility remains that another sudden increase in the number of EEO complaint cases received may be associated with an increase in time that cases are held with IRD without being actively processed.

Recommendations for Addressing Case Backlog

To address case backlog, interviewees discussed increasing the number of mediations and blitzes conducted, which are discussed later. Increasing the number of investigators employed by IRD was also mentioned. One interviewee stated the following:

> Obviously there's an IRD staff issue—whether we have enough people to investigate the cases. I think that needs to be raised as an issue. Investigators now—GS-13 investigators—have eight, ten, 12 cases at a time. They're already juggling the full workload. You can continue to pile on cases to them but they have—they get a certain number of days to complete a case internally. Obviously, as with any process, if you devote more staff, you'll reduce the processing time because you'll have more people focused on that work.

As seen in Figure 4.2 in Chapter Four, IRD investigations are being completed in a timely manner. However, to manage the influx of several hundred cases (e.g., such as in the instance of receipt of a class complaint), temporary employment of more investigators may be worthwhile to consider.

Use of Alternative Dispute Resolution

In addition to describing several of the factors that they perceived as contributing to increasing the amount of time used to process EEO complaint cases, participants also described factors believed to decrease the amount of time used to process cases. One element that participants supported was the use of ADR, also referred to as mediation. When a case is mediated, the relevant parties discuss options that may permit the settlement of a case. If the parties agree to a settlement during this process, the need for a completed investigation is eliminated. Thus, the number of cases requiring completed investigations may be reduced through increased use of ADR. ADR may take place before or after a case is filed with IRD.

In describing approval for ADR, one interviewee commented, "I am a strong proponent of mediation. It's the best thing since Pampers. [There is] always a chance to resolve a case."

Another interviewee stated,

> Mediation is a great tool; it really is—and it cuts down the pro-
> cessing time—once it's mediated, it's done, so it looks good for
> everybody, so it helps the whole picture—so they come together,
> agree, and get done what they need to get done.

A concern with ADR among interviewees was that individuals
within the agencies may not agree to participate in it. If a complainant agrees to participate in ADR but the relevant management does
not, the mediation can be difficult, if not impossible, to facilitate. One
interviewee commented,

> Even when we get a case for investigation, we try to settle it even
> if mediation doesn't work. It is frustrating having agency reps say,
> "oh, I never settle." Not by looking at individual case, just saying,
> "I never settle anything." That is unhelpful when the rep is that
> blatantly unwilling to work with us.

One reason suggested for agencies not participating in ADR is
that they are concerned that employees will perceive the EEO complaint process as an avenue to have their needs met easily. Thus, IRD
employees believe that agencies perceive that increasing ADRs may be
associated with increases in the number of complainants who utilize
the EEO complaint process. For example, an interviewee commented,

> There is still, there are still people within DoD who do not want
> to settle cases. I've heard people say this—they feel that if you
> settle an EEO complaint, you signal that you're willing to give
> money for these complaints, open door for everyone to file a com-
> plaint and hope for money. . . . There's a misperception about set-
> tlement. In activities where they settle a lot, [I] make [the] argu-
> ment [that] all you do is signal that management is perceptive to
> your needs—doesn't mean every employee who works there will
> file EEO complaint. I don't think there's evidence of that. Some
> agencies settle a lot. At every step, alternative dispute resolution
> needs to be, you know, explained. Always in every step, it's a valu-
> able way to approach.

These comments suggest that greater use of ADR may facilitate increases in the observed timeliness of EEO complaint processing. Specifically, increased use of ADR may decrease the number of formal cases filed and number of complaints that need to be processed by IRD. However, additional measures may be needed to promote ADR within DoD, including more strongly promoting or requiring that agencies participate in ADR when a complainant has signaled a willingness to pursue a settlement.

Use of Blitzes

Another option that participants perceive as contributing to improvements in the timeliness of EEO complaint processing was the use of what IRD refers to as blitzes. Currently, IRD may conduct a blitz when there are approximately seven or more formal EEO complaint cases filed with IRD at one location (e.g., one military installation). Upon receiving multiple cases from one location, IRD will work to determine whether the location is willing to participate in a blitz. If so, IRD will work with the EEO office at that location to obtain the necessary documentation and organize a series of interviews with those involved in the complaint cases. These interviews will be scheduled during a set time frame, such as one week. After scheduling, IRD investigators will travel to the location to process the cases in person during the scheduled time frame. Possessing all or most of the appropriate documentation and the ability to conduct the necessary interviews during this set time frame permits IRD to rapidly process, or blitz, these cases.

One interviewee described the blitzes as follows:

> When we do a blitz, the whole point is that the agencies say, "We're ready. If you can get someone here in 30 days, we're good." They're ready for facilitation and getting through the documents. You are expediting and getting through the case pretty quick.

Another interviewee commented,

> You go there; it just makes sense to me. You go there. It worked.
> We were able to knock out a lot of cases quickly, to bring down
> the inventory quite a bit. . . . They wanted a blitz, and we blitzed
> cases, a minimum of seven at once. That was worth the while.

Commenting on why the blitzes are effective, an interviewee
stated,

> I think that the reason it helps is that it gets the cooperation of the
> agency, and we have more support from them to provide docu-
> ments and so forth—they are equally involved with us in getting
> the work out, if you will.

Participants also provided words of caution in terms of the use of
blitzes. Specifically, they noted that "blitz programs monopolize tal-
ented investigators away from other complaints." Further, they noted
that blitzes are less effective for locations with fewer complaints and
limited staff. One interviewee stated,

> If you have smaller numbers and you only have onesies or twosies,
> then they wouldn't support it. Also, there are some agencies where
> they don't have the staffing to help with the EEO arena . . . insuf-
> ficient staff to do a lot of cases at one point in time.

To address the concern of attempting blitzes at locations that have
submitted fewer than seven cases to IRD for processing, IRD may
consider greater utilization of centralized blitzing. If there are several
separate locations within proximity of one another that have submitted cases for investigation, IRD may work with the separate locations
to interview all of the appropriate parties at one central location. The
separate locations would each have their documentation available and
interviews scheduled during one common time frame, and individuals from the separate places would meet with IRD investigators at one
place. One interviewee noted that, although infrequently used, centralized blitzing has been performed by IRD previously.

Summary of IRD Perceptions of Processing Timeliness

IRD personnel provided several areas of consideration for improving the timeliness of processing EEO complaints. Due to the perceived delays in processing that are stimulated by lack of necessary data and documentation from agencies, facilitation of data and documentation submission through increased accountability or standardization was suggested. One way to promote accountability and standardization may be through use of checklists. To address perceived delays caused by the lack of experience among intake review staff, interviewees suggested hiring more-experienced individuals for intake review or eliminating intake review altogether. The employment of more investigators was one option interviewees suggested for addressing case backlog. They also suggested increased promotion and use of ADR, which may be accomplished through a requirement for management. Notably, the ability to require management to participate in ADR may be dependent on the establishment of common ADR regulations that also abide by appropriate legal requirements among DoD components. Continued use of blitzes may also facilitate increases in EEO complaint processing timeliness.

CHAPTER SIX

Perceptions of and Potential Avenues for Improving Timeliness of EEO Complaint Processing in the Military Services

After interviewing IRD personnel, we conducted interviews with EEO directors of the military services and personnel at EEO field offices for the services. During these interviews, we posed questions regarding interviewees' thoughts on the initial improvement themes that arose during interviews with IRD personnel. Interviewees were also asked questions regarding additional ideas for improving the timeliness of EEO complaint processing.

Service Perceptions of Processing Timeliness

To assess perceptions of EEO formal complaint processing timeliness, we interviewed 11 individuals involved with supervising or conducting the EEO complaint process in the Air Force, Army, and Navy. To obtain a list of personnel at military service EEO offices who could be interviewed for this project, we asked the EEO directors of the military services' EEO complaint processes to provide the names, email addresses, and phone numbers of individuals willing and able to provide their thoughts regarding the current process and potential adjustments that may be made to improve the timeliness of EEO complaints in DoD. Upon receiving a list of individuals, a RAND researcher emailed the individuals, requesting their participation in telephone interviews and providing a brief description of the project and the topics that would be addressed during the interviews. During the winter of 2013, phone interviews were scheduled with those who agreed to participate.

Each interview lasted approximately 45 to 60 minutes. During the interview, either a graduate student or research assistant recorded notes. As with the interviews conducted with IRD personnel, all participants were informed that notes would be taken during interviews and that they had the right to refuse to participate or answer any question. The personnel who were interviewed described their job positions as follows: one Air Force base director of EO and dispute resolution, one Air Force base strategic adviser for EO, one Air Force base EEO officer, two Army fort EEO managers, three Army fort EEO officers, one Navy deputy EEO officer, one Navy EEO complaint manager, and one Navy fleet EEO program director.

As with the interviews conducted with IRD personnel, interviewees were asked questions regarding their perceptions of the speed of formal EEO complaint processing. Specifically, they were asked which parts of the process move the most slowly and which parts move the most quickly. They were also asked about submission of documents to IRD; about the potential use of checklists, mediations, and blitzes; and for additional recommendations for improvements that could be made to increase the timeliness of the process.

Delays in Data and Documentation Submission

When asked which parts of the EEO complaint process tend to move most slowly, interviewees commented that collecting the necessary documentation required a lengthy period of time. This source of delay was also observed by IRD personnel. One aspect that interviewees among the military services perceived as contributing to data and documentation delays was the receipt of requested documents from HR and relevant offices. One Army interviewee stated,

> It depends on whether or not the activities understand the importance of the document requests. Some of them don't understand the sense of urgency we have to respond to document request, because this is all time-driven. We are either going to do the request for investigation without the documentation, saying [the] agency didn't reply to doc request when requested, or we will

delay that process working with the activity sometimes down to the wire.

Another Army interviewee commented on interference from legal personnel. To ensure that the complaint process continues in a legally acceptable manner, legal personnel may be used to review complaints or documentation. However, during informal and initial formal complaint processing, litigation is not to occur. One interviewee commented that these guidelines are not always followed:

> We in EEO run into problems gathering documents that we can't get without assistance. In the field, there are issues with personnel offices. We also have issues with legal office trying to entrench themselves into the precomplaint part—they start litigating. That can preclude getting documents to get to IRD early on.

Interviewees also noted that there is variability in the extent to which EEO officers refer to the IRD website for determining the documentation to submit to the IRD with a request for investigation. Although some utilize the website document lists, others may not. One Navy interviewee noted,

> I think they call it IRD's suggested documents list; whether that's used is dependent on the supervisor in the EEO office—the consistency of how that's used varies.

To assist in promoting their EEO office timeliness and in receiving increased guidance regarding the documents needed by IRD, interviewees also noted that they would purposely submit incomplete EEO case files to IRD. One Navy individual noted, "I would rather have an incomplete case rather than a complete case that is late." An Army interviewee stated,

> But we kind of cut corners to stay timely. Maybe they're taking 45 days because they're reading the checklists and turning them in. I don't know. I don't know which is better. But with Army, it's 15 days that I'm up against.

One Air Force interviewee commented on the utility of an explicit document request from IRD:

> Lots of folks want to file complaints; lots of folks don't want to give you information. Getting info from complainants is almost impossible. When you have an IRD request—a document request from IRD—there are some teeth there. There are some by-law requirements that they're required to respond to it and provide it.

Perceptions of Use of Checklists

To address concerns regarding document and data submission to IRD, interviewees were asked about the potential benefits and drawbacks of the future use of document checklists. They were informed that these checklists might build from the current document lists on the IRD website. They were told that, if the checklists were implemented, those submitting case files to IRD might be required to submit the applicable checklists, indicating which of the listed documents were and were not being submitted. If documents were not submitted, the individual would include explanation for the omissions.

Interviewees noted benefits of the checklists. For example, one Navy individual stated,

> I think the checklists are very worthwhile—to go on the website and pull out exactly what's needed. It takes the guesswork out of what's needed for that particular complaint.

An Army interviewee stated,

> I support the checklists. I would submit checklists. Check off, sign document, whatever. So I hope that will alleviate IRD coming back, asking for same documents. I hope that's the intent.

Further commenting on the checklists, an Air Force interviewee stated,

> Absolutely. Make them do it. . . . IRD has that guideline. Ask the complainant or management, it's not that difficult.

Concerns were raised regarding whether IRD would abide by the checklists or consistently request additional documentation not contained within the checklists. In response to the potential future use of checklists, one Army interviewee stated,

> We're kind of doing that now. We look at the lists of what they want. And we're trying to do that, but they still always ask for more. Sometimes it's—doesn't seem to be consistent. In one case, ask for this; in another one, same issue, something else. But we're six months into a complaint by then.

Interviewees also noted that it may be difficult to develop checklists that are appropriate for all cases involving certain bases or issues. One Army interviewee commented,

> My concern with checklists and timing is that those lists don't help in some cases. Hostile work environment claims—checklist, other than org chart/titles, that's about it that's standard. Everything else is really unique to the situation.

An Air Force interviewee noted,

> When we send that checklist to management, we have to go through it and say, "that doesn't pertain to you, that doesn't pertain to you." The issue is so different that one standard checklist is almost a waste of time.

Overall, these comments suggest that the military services perceive that there are issues with timeliness of data and document submission to IRD. If checklists can be developed that contain all or most of the documents that IRD will need to process a case, the services may be willing to use these lists to assist with document submission.

Delays Due to Limited Experience of IRD Intake Personnel

Several interviewees also mentioned concerns regarding their interactions with IRD. Although many spoke positively regarding their interactions with their IRD service component managers, they expressed frustration in dealing with other personnel. Interviewees specifically referenced intake when describing their frustrations, which complements concerns expressed by IRD personnel regarding this aspect of EEO complaint processing. For example, one Army interviewee commented,

> Sometimes when [IRD] personnel ask for stuff, they don't know what they're asking for. . . . We have to review document requests to determine if it's necessary. Sometimes we can go through it easily—requested 45 documents, half aren't applicable. . . . I think it's expedience. Person doing document requests is probably not—they're probably clerical, not that familiar with it.

A Navy interviewee stated,

> I know there were some issues with intake and investigation, where the investigator would say, "This is everything I need," . . . and they send us everything we already sent them. That's very frustrating and that's happened a lot. They will say, "we never got that." "What do you mean? I confirmed with intake that you got that." That's not my problem. I don't want to be snarky with investigators, but what's the use of having an uploading system if you're not going to be using them?

Similarly, a Navy individual noted,

> I would think as long as we do what we need to do to assure everything IRD requires, they could do a very good job by looking closely at the case file that's forwarded to them before they send out an additional doc request to make sure the document that they are looking for is not actually there. Don't hold up our process when the docs were there the entire time.

These comments suggest that the EEO offices perceive that IRD intake personnel are asking for unnecessary documentation or documentation that has already been submitted. Participants did not suggest changes to make to address their concerns regarding IRD intake.

As noted later, potential ways to address this include changing the required qualification for intake personnel, eliminating intake review, or use of checklists.

Delays Due to Case Backlog

Interviewees also commented on their awareness of the case backlog experienced by IRD. They suggested that this backlog may be the cause for a lack of timeliness in processing. One Navy interviewee commented,

> I would like to see that they review that sooner. I understand they're back-logged, but ideally if they reviewed it in a week and they asked for something, we could jump on it right then versus waiting three months down the road.

An Army interviewee noted,

> I understand the backlog, but it's very frustrating. We're held accountable for IRD.

These comments suggest that case backlog is primarily a concern that is associated with reduced processing timeliness at IRD, and not the agencies.

Use of Alternative Dispute Resolution

Participants were also asked to provide their perceptions of ADR, or mediation. Specifically, they were asked the benefits and drawbacks of the use of ADR. Interviewees spoke very positively about ADR. For example, one Navy interviewee noted,

> I think overall mediation is good, because it gets people talking. It, depending on where you are, if you pull a number of supervisors and ask if they want to mediate, the majority would say no,

and I think that's because they don't understand the process, I think they look at it as if they're being forced to do something.

Currently, ADR is a voluntary process in which complainants and management may either agree or decline to participate. To further promote ADR, participants were asked whether it may be worthwhile to require that management participate in ADR if complainants have signaled their own willingness to participate. Participants spoke positively of taking this measure, and some indicated that their own commands already required that management participate in ADR. For example, one Army interviewee commented,

> Big advocate for mediation. I know what it does. Saves time, money, resources—gets them to do what they were required to do. Yes it needs to be—a policy that if employee wants to participate, management must participate. Some commands have that policy now, but not across the board. If the complainant chooses to mediate, management should participate.

Another Army interviewee stated,

> Yes. It's mandatory within the garrison here. Highly recommended by our two-star. Generally if they balk, I tell them, "Do you realize the two-star highly encourages that? I think I have to call him and tell him this." I've never had anyone—never been in situation where they've refused. We have good luck with that here.

One Air Force interviewee specifically commented on the extent to which requirements can motivate participation, noting,

> I think that if you do have those few managers that don't want to participate, because they feel they're right, we can try to tell them, the mediator tries to make them look at other things. Management, when they hear they're required to do something by law, normally they pay attention.

Interviewees also provided suggestions and points to keep in mind in terms of the potential implementation of required mediation among management. Specifically, they noted that when immediate management refuses to participate, higher-level management may participate instead in mediation. One Navy interviewee stated,

> I think that there should be a caveat, basically, that—I do like how the Navy has it set up. They have to provide a reason if they're not going to, because management has to think about it and run it though the commanding officer. The commanding officer needs a good reason to sign his name off on it. I think that's really the way to go.

An Army interviewee stated,

> Typically we move up a level of supervision. When we mediate, we try to resolve complaint if we can—but if we do formal mediation, we bring a second-level supervisor in. This is designed to say that the agency is committed to resolution at the earliest levels. Second, we want to make sure the employee feels heard by the chain of command. There is a little heartburn by first-line supervisor who says, "That wasn't my intention." But we get two managers talking to each other during the process, so the first one won't not agree to do the settlement. We move up the level of authority. This enhances the employee's willingness to do it: "I'm not just across from my aggressor. I get to tell my story to someone who can fix it."

Others noted the importance of educating management on the utility of ADR. For example, one Navy interviewee commented,

> I would keep in mind that you might find some push back from managers who don't necessarily see that as a benefit. Again, it goes back to the mind-set and how people view the ADR process. If you implement it, it will need to be followed up with some education as to why ADR is important to the federal government. Reducing cost, time away from office . . . etc.

Use of Blitzes

In addition to providing their perceptions of ADR, participants were also asked to provide their thoughts on the use of blitzes to process cases. Not every interviewee had participated in a blitz, but those who had participated generally spoke positively regarding the ability of blitzes to facilitate rapid processing. However, they also noted that the blitzes were difficult on their labor attorneys. An Air Force interviewee noted,

> The blitzes are great and they should stick with that if they can knock out five cases at a time. One time we had someone do six, which was excellent. It wore the labor attorney out. Legal was shocked that they were doing them all, but when we explained why, it seemed to work. She was kind of tired and had to do a lot of preparation. Don't tell me in two weeks that you're going to do a blitz. Give us at least three to four weeks for the labor attorney to prepare. If they give enough time it works great, but if they don't give enough time, I don't feel they . . . the labor attorney shouldn't do that much.

An Army interviewee commented,

> My attorneys didn't like it. But it helped me out tremendously, and [An IRD staff member] is for this—to stay ahead. There's a lot of risk in not utilizing that resource. . . Build it into the process—then it's already formatted, and we're not waiting until 180 days and asking for a 90-day extension to extend the process.

The military service EEO offices supported the use of blitzes to rapidly process cases. However, interviewees recommended that sufficient time be provided to collect documentation and schedule interviews, thereby reducing the chances of overwhelming labor attorneys.

Hostile Work Environment Claims

Several participants among the military service EEO offices commented on the complexity of cases with certain characteristics, explicitly mentioning cases in which complainants indicate they have been working in hostile work environments. They noted that these cases can be difficult and untimely to process, because complainants indicate a diversity of discriminatory behaviors within these claims. They also indicated that a large number of complaints are now being filed under hostile work environment claims. For example, one Army interviewee noted, "I would say [that] one in every four cases I accept is hostile work environment." A Navy interviewee commented,

> That's a black box and a larger number of cases are being filed under hostile work environment. And there's a lot of uncertainty and confusion as what's getting filed under hostile work environment.

Another interviewee also noted that complaints are being described as hostile work environment when it is unclear how to frame them. Rather than allow the possibility of the EEOC later requiring an agency to process a rejected case that did not clearly possess a particular issue or set of issues, the office will simply accept the case and file it under hostile work environment. This Air Force interviewee stated:

> If we can't find where to put it, to keep EEOC from demanding it, we put it under hostile work environment. We will put the other issues there and tie them to an employment action. If it's true, what would it take to resolve this? Sometimes, it's just hard to explain a hostile work environment. If that is discriminatory, what are you benefiting from for us resolving this? Nothing? But EEOC demanded it—if they state hostile work environment, we just put it under there.

In describing complaints involving hostile work environment claims, one Navy interviewee also stated,

> What is a hostile work environment? Well that's basically what it is. Any complaint filed regardless of the basis, they will say hostile work environment, and what it comes down to is you have a loss in communication or lack of communication between the complainant and management or complainant and another coworker.

> The manager is still responsible for behavior in the workplace. It's a degrading of communication. . . . When management fails to take action, it creates a hostile work environment. It can fall into any of the bases.

These comments suggest that additional assessment of complaints that are being filed under hostile work environment may be worthwhile. Specifically, interviewees expressed confusion regarding these claims but also noted that the numbers of complaints involving this claim are increasing.

Summary of Military Service Perceptions of Processing Timeliness

Many of the comments provided by military service personnel complemented and provided additional detail regarding the areas of consideration mentioned by IRD personnel. Like IRD personnel, the military services perceived delays in processing to be stimulated by lack of necessary data and documentation. They noted that it can be difficult for the EEO officers to obtain requisite documentation from relevant parties, and it can be difficult to establish what documents are needed by IRD. The military service personnel also indicated that IRD intake staff will often ask for documentation that has already been submitted. One way to reduce the number of requests made by IRD may be through use of checklists, such that staff will have explicit information regarding the documentation that has been submitted. Military service personnel also spoke positively about the use of mediations and the potential future requirement that management either participate in mediation or provide higher-level management a reason for refusal to participate. Finally, continued use of blitzes to facilitate increases in EEO complaint processing timeliness was also supported.

CHAPTER SEVEN

Randomized Control Trial Design to Assess Checklist Implementation

The comments received from IRD and military service EEO personnel during interviews with the RAND team suggested potential changes that may be made to the current EEO formal complaint process in DoD. For example, the implementation of checklists may be one avenue to pursue as part of efforts to improve timeliness in processing. Changes in processing should include evaluations of the impacts of these changes.[1] After implementation, a thoughtfully designed evaluation can help determine whether a particular processing change is worthwhile to maintain and whether additional modifications should be pursued. A well-designed study may facilitate assessment of the potential effects that changes made to EEO complaint processing can have on the timeliness of EEO complaints in DoD.

An RCT is considered to be one of the most rigorous ways of assessing the effects of a treatment.[2] An RCT is a study design that involves random assignment of entities into either a group that receives an intervention (i.e., a treatment group), which may involve implementing a change in EEO complaint processing, or a group that receives no intervention (i.e., a control group), which may involve continuing to use the current steps and measures to process EEO cases. After study implementation, differences between these groups in terms of

---

[1] Peter H. Rossi, Mark W. Lipsey, and Howard E. Freeman, *Evaluation: A Systematic Approach,* 7th ed., Thousand Oaks, Calif.: Sage Publications, 2003.

[2] Bonnie Sibbald and Roland Martin, "Understanding Controlled Trials: Why Are Randomised Controlled Trials Important?" *British Medical Journal,* Vol. 316, No. 7126, January 17, 1998, p. 201.

the outcomes of interest may be attributed to the differences in treatment between the groups.[3] Specific outcomes of interest include the following: time with initial agency, time with IRD intake, and time with IRD investigations. An RCT may be used to assess the effects of changes made to DoD EEO complaint processing, particularly in terms of the implementation of checklists.

There are limitations to the RCT study design. In addition to requiring the abilities to randomly assign entities to certain conditions, carefully implement a treatment, and closely monitor the treatment and control groups, RCTs require that researchers have the ability to collect data on the variables of interest in a study, such as outcome variables of relevance to processing timeliness. In fall of 2013, IRD began to implement a new database to collect and maintain data regarding EEO complaint cases. The implementation of this new database prevented IRD from incorporating additional variables that IRD and military EEO service personnel perceived as important to observe within an RCT involving assessment of the effects of EEO complaint processing changes.[4] During the transition of IRD and military service personnel from using the old EEO complaint case database to using the new database, educating personnel on the new database, and addressing issues that arose with the new database, IRD resources were limited, and the addition of more data fields to the appropriate databases for the purpose of an RCT was not believed to be feasible.[5]

Further, implementation of the new database may have reduced the ability to assess the effect of the change in processing.[6] Specifically, implementation of the new database at the same time as implementation of another change to processing would make it difficult to

---

[3]   William D.Crano and Marilynn B. Brewer, *Principles and Methods of Social Research*, 2nd ed., Oxford, UK: Psychology Press, 2002.

[4]   Information regarding the new database was obtained from discussions with IRD leadership and EEO program leadership in the ODMEO.

[5]   Information regarding the feasibility of changes to the old and new databases was obtained via email correspondence with IRD leadership.

[6]   Robert Rosenthal and Ralph L. Rosnow, *Essentials of Behavioral Research: Methods and Data Analysis*, 3rd ed., New York: McGraw-Hill, 2007.

determine the true effect of the intervention, such that the effect realized when everyone is adjusting to a new system may not be the same as the effect at full implementation. Due to concerns regarding the implementation of an RCT during FY 2014, the ODMEO, IRD, and military service EEO personnel indicated that a delay in implementation was needed. Thus, this chapter outlines the potential design of an RCT involving checklists but does not describe an implemented RCT.

Use of RCT to Assess Potential Effects of Checklists

Personnel at IRD and the military services discussed different potential processing changes during their interviews, including the implementation of checklists to facilitate accountability and standardization in data and document submission. An RCT appeared to be appropriate to use in assessing the potential effects of the implementation of checklists. Specifically, an RCT involves researcher-established variations in the conditions to which groups are exposed. Thus, it involves exposing different groups to different treatment conditions. In discussions with ODMEO and IRD personnel, it was noted that the use of checklists might be implemented among certain entities but not among others. Thus, assignment of entities to a treatment group that used checklists and a control group that did not use checklists was suggested.

By contrast, the implementation of required mediation among management, changes in IRD intake staffing, and continuation of blitzes are processing elements that would each require implementation across all agencies and activities in DoD. Therefore, alternative study designs would need to be considered for assessment of the potential effects of these processing changes. It is worth nothing that, although an RCT may not be suitable for assessment of DoD-wide processing changes, this does not eliminate the possibility of evaluating the potential effects that these changes may have on the timeliness of EEO complaint processing. Alternative designs, such as various quasi-experimental designs, may instead be explored as study design options. However, thorough descriptions of alternative study designs are beyond the scope of this chapter, which focuses on checklist implementation and RCTs.

Assignment to Conditions

To implement an RCT, the units that are to be assigned to either a treatment condition or a control condition must be determined. Ideally, any one EEO complaint case that is filed would be randomly assigned to either a condition in which the EEO officer uses the checklists or a condition in which that same EEO officer does not use the checklists for that particular case. However, it may be difficult and confusing for one individual to process certain cases one way and other cases in a different way, and using the same EEO officer would create contamination across conditions. Further, random assignment of certain EEO officers at a location to utilize the checklists and other EEO officers at that location to not utilize the checklists may also be confusing and would create a strong potential for contamination across study conditions. For example, awareness that certain EEO officers at a location are using checklists may contribute to other EEO officers who had been assigned to the control condition at that location seeking out and using the checklists. Taking all that into account, it was recommended that locations be assigned to either a treatment condition involving the use of checklists or a control condition that continued to process cases utilizing the old document lists on the IRD website.[7]

Next, the different military services process cases differently. One military installation may have multiple activities that process EEO complaints. For example, one Army base may have several activities to which different individuals may go to file an EEO complaint case. In the Army and Air Force, the different EEO activities at each installation go through a centralized process at the installation. As such, after an individual has filed a case at a certain installation's activity,

---

[7] Information regarding feasible units to utilize in random assignment to conditions was obtained from discussions with IRD leadership and EEO program leadership in the ODMEO.

the activity subsequently submits the case to a centralized installation office to continue through EEO complaint processing. Again, this centralized process occurs only at the Army and Air Force installations. In contrast, activities at the Navy installations operate independently and do not go through a centralized installation office.[8]

The centralized process at Army and Air Force installations may influence the extent to which different activities may maintain different processing conditions. Specifically, military service EEO directors and EEO program leadership in the ODMEO noted that Army and Air Force activities at a particular installation share resources and thus may be likely to share checklists, even if the activities were assigned to different conditions involving using or not using checklists. Given that, contamination across study conditions (i.e., a condition using checklists and a condition not using checklists) would be likely among Army and Air Force activities at a particular installation. Thus, Army and Air Force installations would be assigned to either a treatment condition that was to use checklists or a control condition that was not to use checklists. In other words, all of the activities at a particular Army or Air Force installation would be assigned to the same study condition. In contrast, Navy activities would be assigned to separate conditions. Thus, Navy activities at one installation could be assigned to different conditions. Some installations jointly house different services, and these installation and their corresponding activities should not be included in this proposed study. Further, activities and locations from agencies that are not part of the military services should not be included in this proposed study. This assignment of installations or activities to study conditions reflects the requirements stipulated by military service EEO directors and EEO program leadership in the ODMEO during interviews and discussions.

Using the proposed units (i.e., installations for Air Force and Army and activities for Navy), random assignment to two different

---

[8] Information on centralized processing was obtained from interviews and discussions with military service EEO directors and EEO program leadership in the ODMEO. Before implementation of an RCT, consideration should be given to the most recent processing structure in place at Army, Air Force, and Navy installations.

groups would be conducted. These groups could then be assigned to be the treatment group that utilized checklists or the control group that did not utilize checklists. For Army and Air Force installations, each installation would be randomly assigned to one of two groups (with a probability of 0.5 of being placed in either of the groups). For the Navy, activities, rather than installations, would be assigned to one of two groups.

Checklist Materials

In addition to determining which units to assign to conditions, the materials to be used in the treatment condition (i.e., checklist condition) in this proposed study have also been developed. IRD currently has a list of documents that it requests be submitted with certain cases when a request for investigation is filed. There are separate lists for cases involving different characteristics, including the following: awards, change to lower grade, classification, constructive discharge, denial of detail or reassignment, denial of request for training, disability accommodation, disciplinary actions, sexual harassment, nonsexual harassment, nonreferral, nonselection or nonpromotion, performance-based actions, performance rating, reduction in force, security clearances, termination due to probationary or trial period, termination of temporary term employee, and time and attendance issues. IRD leadership indicated that these document lists were comprehensive and accurate and should be the bases for checklists.

In transitioning the IRD document lists into checklists, several changes were made. Specifically, IRD contact information and instructions were included at the top of each list. In addition, a field was included next to each document in each list that EEO officers would initial to indicate inclusion of that document in the submitted request for investigation case file. A second field was included under each document listed that EEO officers would use to explain why a document listed is not being submitted. At the end of each list, four fields were included. One field was to be completed if additional documents beyond those contained in the list were included. Another field was to be used to print the name of the EEO specialist or manager submitting the request for investigation. The third field was to be signed by the EEO specialist or manager submitting the request for investigation. The fourth field was to be used to provide the date on which the request for investigation was being submitted. The appendix, available separately online, contains copies of all checklists. These will need to be continuously updated in order to include documents that are frequently requested and exclude documents that are not needed by investigators.

These checklists differ from the current document lists on the IRD website. They increase accountability of those submitting data and documents to IRD, such that submitters must provide their initials and signatures on the checklists. In addition, unlike the current IRD document lists, all appropriate case-relevant checklists are to be submitted with requests for investigation, which may permit IRD personnel to more easily determine which documentation is and is not present in a file.

Checklist Use

Required Use of Checklists

During our interviews with IRD and military service EEO personnel, a concern that was raised regarding the current document lists contained on the IRD website was that use of the document lists is variable across EEO personnel. It follows that simply asking those assigned to the treatment condition to use the checklists may be unlikely to result in consistent use of the checklists across individuals, activities, installations, and agencies. We held discussions with IRD leadership and IRD intake management to determine feasible avenues to pursue in promoting checklist use among those in the treatment condition.

One option would be for IRD intake to return requests for investigation to those in the treatment condition who do not submit checklists. However, IRD personnel expressed concern regarding the reactions that they would receive regarding the return of otherwise-complete requests for investigation that did not contain checklists. Thus, an alternative option was established. Using this alternative option, IRD would hold requests for investigation that were received from those in the treatment condition who submitted cases without checklists. IRD intake would inform those who submitted the case that checklists were needed, and the case would not be processed until these checklists were received.

Availability of Checklists

Installations and activities in the different conditions must have differential access to the current IRD document lists or new checklists. Thus, two web pages will be needed: one that contains the current IRD document lists and another that contains the new checklists. To provide access to the appropriate web page, a drop-down menu listing all activities and installations can be included on the IRD website. Depending on whether they are assigned to the treatment or control condition, those who select a particular activity or installation would be directed to a page that contains either the current IRD document lists or the new checklists.[9] As discussed below, checklist use may be tracked in the IRD database.

Notification of Study

All IRD and EEO personnel within the military services would need to be informed of a study examining EEO complaint procedures and processing time. To inform military service EEO personnel of this study, a notification may be placed on the IRD website. Individuals who visit the IRD website would see this notification. Further, an email sent jointly by the ODMEO and IRD would be sent to all military service EEO personnel at least one month before study implementation. Another reminder email would be sent two weeks before implementation, and a final email would be sent one week before implementation. This email would provide the purpose of the study, ways in which installations and activities would be affected, and contact information that may be used by those with questions or concerns.

---

[9]   Via email communication, IRD leadership indicated that this change to the IRD website was feasible.

Data Collection

To be able to assess the potential effectiveness of new checklists, consistent information regarding several variables of interest will need to be collected by IRD for each case submitted to IRD. The requisite information is listed in Table 7.1 and contains the variables that military ser-

Table 7.1
Variables to Be Collected for All Formal EEO Complaint Cases

Variables	Collected by IRD as of December 2013
Agency	√
Installation	√
Activity	√
Date case formally filed with activity	√
Date case filed with IRD intake	√
Intake person's identifying information	√
Date case filed with IRD investigation	√
Date ROI completed	√
Date ROI mailed	√
Issues filed with case (separate field for each issue)	√
Whether complete checklist, incomplete checklist, or no checklist filed for each issue (separate field for each issue)	
Name of person who signed checklist for each issue	
Bases filed with case (separate field for each basis)	√
Dates of amendments filed with case	√
Intake person's identifying information for each amendment	√
Documents requested by IRD intake (separate field for each document, including checklists)	
Date of IRD document request (separate field for each document)	
Date of document receipt of requested documents (separate field for each document)	

vice EEO personnel, IRD leadership, and ODMEO EEO leadership indicated would need to be assessed in terms of thoroughly evaluating the effects of checklists. Most of these variables are already collected by IRD. However, several additional variables will need to be added to the IRD database. Further, IRD personnel will need to be trained on how to enter data into the new fields and how to differentially process cases from installations and activities in the treatment and control conditions.

Additional Variables

To permit tracking of checklist use, additional fields addressing whether the appropriate checklists were submitted with a request for investigation will need to be added to the IRD database. These fields would be completed for all cases, regardless of whether the request for investigation has been submitted by an installation or activity in a treatment or control condition. This completion of checklist fields for all cases would permit assessment of whether those in the control condition did not submit checklists, which would be in alignment with the proposed study design, and it would also permit assessment of whether those in the treatment condition submitted complete checklists.

To permit rapid assessment of who is submitting checklists, additional fields will need to be added to capture the name of the person submitting each checklist. These fields will permit assessment of who should be contacted regarding the documents submitted for each issue. In terms of analyses, these fields will permit assessment and identification of individuals who are consistently submitting complete or incomplete checklists. This may facilitate accountability in submission of requests for investigation.

Further, data fields should also be added to permit systematic tracking of document requests. Specifically, a separate field should be completed for each document that IRD requests from an EEO office. In addition, fields capturing the date of request for each requested document and date of document receipt for each requested document should also be added. The addition of these fields will permit determination of which documents are frequently requested and whether EEO offices are able to submit these in a timely manner. These fields will also permit assessment of whether the use of checklists is associated with lower numbers of requested documents.[10]

Multiple data analysis options may be used to assess the effect of treatment. For example, the simplest initial option may be to use independent sample t-tests, or bivariate regression analyses, comparing treatment and control groups on time with initial agency, time with IRD intake, and time with IRD investigators. Additional analyses (e.g., analyses of variance) may compare differences in time with each element (i.e., initial agency, IRD intake, IRD investigations) between treatment and control groups across DoD agencies. Further, analyses involving only the treatment group may also be conducted. These include, for example, examining the association between submission of a complete checklist, incomplete checklist, or no checklist on time with each element. Assessments may also be conducted on the length of time required to process cases by each IRD intake person. Further, more-sophisticated regression structures incorporating baseline covariates or correlational structures may also be appropriate.

Stakeholder Support

When implementing this proposed study, or any other study, it is important to include stakeholders, because they may determine the success or failure of a research effort. Stakeholders have been defined as follows:

> Individuals, groups, or organizations having a significant interest in how well a program functions, for instance, those with decision-

---

[10] The time period during which data should be collected will depend on the strength of the effect of checklists. If using checklists increases or reduces total processing time by 10 percent or more, a difference is very likely to be shown in a data collection period as short as six months, even if complaint levels remain at the low level seen in the latter half of FY 2012. However, if true differences are as small as 5 percent, picking up on this would require between a year and a year and a half of data collection.

making authority over the program, funders, sponsors, administrators and personnel, and clients or intended beneficiaries.[11]

Before study implementation, information regarding all logistical details of the study will need to be discussed with military service EEO directors, IRD leadership, IRD intake management, and ODMEO EEO program leadership. These are relevant stakeholders who have been included in the design of this proposed study. These stakeholders will also need to be included in the implementation of the study. Other stakeholders to consider consulting before study implementation include, but are not limited to, the following: IRD investigators, IRD intake staff, military service diversity program directors, and nonmilitary DoD agency EEO directors.

Limitations

Any research effort has limitations. Even if this study is implemented exactly as planned and without any difficulties, this proposed study design is not without limitations. In order to process cases received from those in treatment and control conditions differently, IRD personnel will need to know whether the case has been submitted by an installation or activity in a treatment or control condition. This personnel awareness of conditions may affect the time IRD personnel use to process cases. Thus, awareness of conditions, rather than treatment differences between conditions, may affect potential differences between groups in processing timeliness.

In addition, awareness among personnel at different installations and activities that they are in a study may lead to differences in EEO complaint processing among these personnel. This is known as the Hawthorne effect, or observer effect. Specifically, participants' awareness that they are in a study or experiment may lead them to modify their behavior from what it would have been without awareness

---

[11] Rossi, Lipsey, and Freeman, 2003.

of the study or experiment.[12] Thus, changes in the processing behaviors of military service EEO personnel may occur simply because of their awareness that a study is being conducted. Although stakeholders may want to withhold information that a study is being conducted, this may not be feasible. Those in different EEO offices in the same or different services communicate with one another, and they will likely learn about the study or be able to ascertain that a study is being conducted, even if they are not informed directly.

Summary

An RCT study design may be used to assess the effects that checklist implementation could have on EEO complaint processing in DoD. Even if not used for checklist implementation, this general study design may be modified to permit evaluation of alternative processing changes involving random assignment of units to different treatment conditions. By using a well-designed and carefully implemented RCT, a clearer understanding of the impact of processing changes may be achieved.

---

[12] John G. Adair, "The Hawthorne Effect: A Reconsideration of the Methodological Artifact," *Journal of Applied Psychology,* Vol. 69, No. 2, 1984, pp. 334–345.

CHAPTER EIGHT

Conclusion and Recommendations for Formal EEO Complaint Processing in DoD

This research effort sought to identify ways to improve the timeliness of EEO complaint processing. To do so, we obtained detailed information about DoD's EEO complaint process through discussions of policy and practice with key personnel and through review of previous research, namely the FY 2012 LSS evaluation. These sources of information suggested that the military service EEO personnel and IRD personnel held concerns regarding current aspects of EEO complaint processing. These concerns included lack of training and mentoring for those in the services who are processing formal complaints, lack of IRD intake training competency, perceptions of poor communication and collaboration between IRD and the military services, and lack of standardization of the EEO complaint process and forms.

In addition, we assessed recent trends and patterns of formal EEO complaint cases through use of EEOC and IRD data. Further, we used IRD case history data to identify key characteristics and processing timeliness of EEO complaints. These data suggested that the timeliness of EEO complaint processing has not declined due to changes in caseload or changes in case complexity. Resource issues, such as staff number and competency, may influence timeliness. However, data on resources do not allow adequate assessment of their influence.

Based on the information we obtained and assessed, we offer several recommendations to improve the timely processing of formal EEO complaints in DoD, which may assist DoD in meeting EEOC regulations. Two of these recommendations involve ways to address current case backlog and reduce the potential for future backlog, and two involve changes that may be made to address aspects of current processing that may contribute to delays in formal EEO complaint processing. We also offer a fifth recommendation that addresses the need to systematically implement and evaluate processing changes.

Addressing Case Backlog

Interviews and discussions with IRD personnel and military service personnel involved with the EEO process revealed concerns regarding a backlog of cases at IRD. Specifically, a sharp increase in the number of cases received by IRD was noted as contributing to difficulties in processing EEO complaint cases in a timely manner. These discussions also revealed ways to address case backlog, which inform our recommendations.

Recommendation 1: Continue to Blitz Cases

To address case backlog, DoD should continue to utilize the process that IRD has termed "blitz." The blitz is a process that personnel at the military services and IRD have already been using, albeit on a somewhat limited basis. Specifically, installations that have seven or more cases have been considered as candidates for this blitz process. When an installation participates in a blitz, it collects all necessary documentation and schedules interviews with all relevant individuals during a limited time frame. Afterwards, one or more IRD investigators will visit the installation in person and rapidly process the cases.

Those involved with the blitzes spoke positively about the ability of this process to increase the rapidity of investigations. Indeed, blitzing the cases may help with quickly reducing backlog and preventing continued backlog. To permit locations with a smaller number of submitted complaints to participate in blitzes, increased utilization of a centralized blitzing process should be pursued. Under a centralized blitzing process, different installations or activities that are in geographic proximity to one another may all collect relevant documentation and schedule relevant interviews during one time frame.[1] This may allow one or more investigators to rapidly process cases that, though not at the same location, are at locations close to one another.

Recommendation 2: Require the Use of Alternative Dispute Resolution Among Management

Another way to reduce backlog is to reduce the number of cases that go to or continue through the formal investigation process. To facilitate this reduction in cases, all agencies within DoD should be required to involve management participation in ADR, or mediation, when the agency has offered ADR and complainants have volunteered to participate in this process. If lower-level management refuses, higher-level management should be consulted.[2] Interviews suggested that several installations already require management participation in ADR. In order for required mediation to be implemented, a DoD mandate that management participate in ADR would be needed. Currently, ADR is recommended by DoD, but it is not always supported by management at particular installations.

Notably, there are instances in which a complainant's immediate manager, or first-level manager, may refuse to participate in ADR or may be inappropriate for it (e.g., sexual harassment claims). In these instances, second- or third-level management should participate in the ADR process instead. If all levels of management refuse to participate, reasons for this refusal should be provided and records of refusal should be maintained. To be clear, our recommendation to require management participation in ADR does not suggest that first-level management must participate. Further, this recommendation

---

[1]   An examination of where military installations in the United States are located shows that approximately one-half of U.S. military installations are within 50 miles of at least one other military installation.

[2]   It was beyond the scope of this project to speak with individual commanders. Thus, we do not have firsthand knowledge of why managers decline to participate in ADR or whether they may feel coerced to participate if their higher-level managers were to participate in their place.

does not suggest that complainants be required to participate in ADR; this is a process in which they must volunteer to participate.[3]

Finally, the Navy requires that management provide an explanation for refusal to participate in ADR. Because of the potential legal implications of this written refusal, we hesitate to recommend written explanation from managers who refuse to participate. For example, there is the potential that a complainant may request the documented explanation for management refusal to participate in ADR, and this documentation may be used against an agency during a trial. However, higher-level management should maintain a record when lower-level management refuses to participate in ADR.

Addressing Current Processing Elements

Steps in the current process appear to require considerable amounts of processing time. Specifically, quantitative and qualitative data suggest that the process of data and document submission to IRD requires a considerable amount of time. To address this, we provide two additional recommendations.

Recommendation 3: Increase Accountability and Standardization of Data and Document Submission Through Use of Checklists

Interviews suggested that incomplete EEO complaint case files are often submitted to IRD with requests for investigation, and time is required to obtain the needed data and documentation for the incomplete cases. Interviewees also noted confusion regarding what to submit with a particular case. In addition, quantitative data obtained from the IRD CaseTrac database showed that cases spent a lengthy period of time with IRD intake. IRD provides a list of required and recommended materials on its website, but whether EEO personnel within the military services access the IRD site and use these lists varies. Further, even when complete cases are submitted to IRD for investiga-

---

[3]   EEOC regulations and procedures are described in 29 CFR, parts 1600 through 1699, and note that ADR is a process in which complainants may volunteer to participate.

tion, documentation already included with the case files is frequently requested by IRD intake staff.

To reduce incomplete case submission and document requests for cases that have been submitted complete, increased accountability and standardization of data and document submission are needed. To accomplish this, IRD should investigate the benefits of requiring submission of checklists with requests for investigation (see the appendix, available separately online at http://www.rand.org/pubs/research_reports/RR680, for example checklists). These checklists require EEO personnel to indicate which documents have and have not been submitted, and they require personnel to attach a name to the document submission. However, before requiring the use of checklists, an RCT should be conducted to assess the potential effects of checklist use on processing timeliness.

Recommendation 4: Employ Experienced or Well-Trained Personnel for IRD Intake

Personnel in IRD and the military services also expressed concerns regarding the qualifications of IRD intake personnel. Specifically, lack of experience among IRD intake staff with the EEO formal complaint process and lack of knowledge regarding the characteristics of EEO complaint cases and documentation needed for these cases were suggested as contributing to delays in EEO complaint processing. To address this aspect of current processing, we recommend that IRD either utilize experienced investigators for the intake of requests for investigation or provide more training to IRD staff employed to intake requests for investigation. Experienced investigators include those who have conducted IRD investigations for several years. Notably, budget restrictions may hinder employment of more-experienced personnel. Whether or not more experienced personnel can be hired in the near future, increased training should remain a priority. If more training is pursued, identifying best practices from the top performers in different positions (e.g., intake, investigators) may assist with training.

A third option for addressing deficits in IRD intake is to eliminate IRD intake review and instead have cases directly transferred to IRD investigators. In that scenario, only IRD investigators would review and organize cases and request files. Although this option is worth considering, the variability in opinions regarding IRD intake staff must be taken into account. Specifically, some IRD personnel noted that the organization of case files and requests for documents by IRD intake prior to provision to investigators was helpful.

Assessing the Impact of Changes

Recommendation 5: Systematically Implement and Evaluate the Effects of Changes to Complaint Processing Procedures

DoD should systematically implement and evaluate any potential changes that it makes in complaint processing procedures. This will facilitate assessment of the effects that these changes have. The most scientifically rigorous way to do this is with an RCT. An RCT is a study design that involves random assignment of entities into either a group that receives a treatment (a treatment group), which may involve implementing a change in EEO complaint processing, or a group that receives no treatment (a control group), which may involve continuing to use the current steps and measures to process EEO cases. After study implementation, differences between these groups in terms of the outcomes of interest, such as complaint processing timeliness, may be attributed to the differences in treatment between the groups.[4]

We recommend that an RCT be conducted to assess the effectiveness of checklists in improving accountability and standardization in data and document submission, and thereby reducing complaint processing times.

---

[4]   Any changes made by specific units during the study period should be noted and reported to IRD or research personnel.

References

Adair, John G., "The Hawthorne Effect: A Reconsideration of the Methodological Artifact," *Journal of Applied Psychology*, Vol. 69, No. 2, 1984, pp. 334–345.

Administrative Dispute Resolution Act of 1996, Public Law 104-320, Title 5, Part 1, Chapter 5, 1996.

Age Discrimination in Employment Act of 1967, Public Law 90-202, *United States Code*, Vol. 29, section 621.

Air Force Instruction 36-2706, *Equal Opportunity Program, Military and Civilian*, October 5, 2010.

Alternative Dispute Resolution Act of 1998, H.R. 3528, Title 28, Part 3, Chapter 44, January 27, 1998.

Americans with Disabilities Act of 1990, Title 1, Public Law 101-336, *United States Code*, Vol. 42, section 12101.

Army Regulation 690-600, *Equal Employment Opportunity Discrimination Complaints*, Washington, D.C.: Headquarters, Department of the Army, February 9, 2004.

Brown, Christopher, *Investigations and Resolutions Directorate Blitz Report: May 23, 2013*, Investigations and Resolutions Division, 2013. Not available to the general public.

Brown, Christopher, and Cathy Janes, *EEO E2E Complaints Process Project*, Investigations and Resolutions Division, 2012. Not available to the general public.

Casella, George, and Roger L. Berger, *Statistical Inference,* 2nd ed., Boston, Mass.: Cengage Learning, 2001.

Civil Rights Act of 1964, Public Law 88-352, Title VII, as amended, in *United States Code*, Vol. 42, section 2000e and following.

Crano, William D., and Marilynn B. Brewer, *Principles and Methods of Social Research*, 2nd ed., Oxford, UK: Psychology Press, 2002.

EEOC—*See* U.S. Equal Employment Opportunity Commission.

Equal Pay Act of 1963, Public Law 88-38, *United States Code*, Vol. 29, section 206(d).

Executive Order 12067, *Providing for Coordination of Federal Equal Employment Opportunity Programs*, June 30, 1978.

Fall Semiannual Regulatory Agenda, FR 77 43498, July 25, 2012.

Genetic Information Nondiscrimination Act of 2008, Public Law 110-233, *United States Code*, Vol. 42, section 2000 and following.

Investigations and Resolutions Division, *Investigations and Resolutions Division Equal Employment Opportunity (EEO) Complaints Process: Rapid Improvement Event (RIE) Final Report*, 2012. Not available to the general public.

IRD—*See* Investigations and Resolutions Division.

MicroPact, web page, Customers tab, 2014. As of October 13, 2014: http://www.entellitrak.com/customers/

Montgomery, Douglas C., Elizabeth A. Peck, and G. Geoffrey Vining, *Introduction to Linear Regression Analysis,* 5th ed., Wiley, 2012.

Rehabilitation Act of 1973, Public Law 93-112, Sections 501 and 505, *United States Code*, Vol. 29, section 791 and following.

Rosenthal, Robert, and Ralph L. Rosnow, *Essentials of Behavioral Research: Methods and Data Analysis*, 3rd ed., New York: McGraw-Hill, 2008.

Rossi, Peter H., Mark W. Lipsey, and Howard E. Freeman, *Evaluation: A Systematic Approach*, 7th ed., Thousand Oaks, Calif.: Sage Publications, 2004.

Sibbald, Bonnie, and Martin Roland, "Understanding Controlled Trials: Why Are Randomised Controlled Trials Important?" *British Medical Journal*, Vol. 316, No. 7126, January 17, 1998, p. 201.

U.S. Air Force, *USAF EEO Lead Time Reduction Event: Rapid Improvement Event (RIE) Final Report*, 2012. Not available to the general public.

U.S. Army, *Army Equal Employment Opportunity (EEO) Complaints Process: Rapid Improvement Event (RIE) Final Report*, 2012. Not available to the general public.

U.S. Department of the Air Force, *Equal Opportunity Program, Military and Civilian,* AFI 36-2706, March 5, 2012.

U.S. Department of Defense Instruction 5010.43, *Implementation and Management of the DoD-Wide Continuous Process Improvement/Lean Six Sigma (CPI/LSS) Program*, July 17, 2009.

U.S. Department of Labor, *Code of Federal Regulations (CFR)*, Title 29—Labor, parts 1600—1699, undated.

U.S. Department of the Navy, *EEO Program Status Report Fiscal Year (FY) 2012,* 2012.

————, Submarine Force U.S. Pacific Fleet, "Individual Discrimination Complaint Process," flow chart, undated.

————, *Civilian Human Resources Manual (DON CHRM)*, January 17, 2003, Chapter 700, Chapter 1600.

————, *Discrimination Complaints Management Manual*, EEO Complaint Process flow chart, June 6, 2008.

U.S. Equal Employment Opportunity Commission, *EEOC Management Directive (MD)-110*, November 9, 1999. As of October 17, 2014:
http://www.eeoc.gov/federal/directives/md110.cfm

————, *EEOC Management Directive (MD)-715*, October 1, 2003. As of October 17, 2014:
http://www.eeoc.gov/federal/directives/md715.cfm

U.S. Government Accountability Office, *Human Capital: Additional Steps Needed to Help Determine the Right Size and Composition of DoD's Total Workforce*, Washington, D.C., GAO-13-470, May 2013.

U.S. Marine Corps, Camp Lejeune, "Civilian Individual Discrimination Complaint Process," flow chart, undated.

U.S. Navy, *Navy Equal Employment Opportunity (EEO) Complaints Process: Rapid Improvement Event (RIE) Final Report*, 2012. Not available to the general public.